# DIALECTICAL BEHAVIOR THERAPY TO THE RESCUE

## TACKLE YOUR BORDERLINE PERSONALITY DISORDER USING DBT SKILLS

### MEGAN SEAL

# CONTENTS

# INTRODUCTION

## A Brief History of DBT

Dialectical Behavior Therapy is a treatment plan that was mainly developed to help people struggling with Borderline Personality Disorder. Dr. Marsha Linehan, the founder of DBT, used to be a firm believer in "regular" Behavioral Therapy and wanted to prove that it could help treat highly suicidal, difficult-to-treat individuals. Little did she know at the time her research study commenced at the University of Washington that traditional Behavioral Therapy would be *completely ineffective* for these individuals. To make things worse, through the course of the study, the participants felt like they were being blamed or told that they themselves were the problem (Duckworth, 2015).

Through trial and error, Marsha eventually added a very important component to the therapy mix - acceptance. She took a leave and studied with a Zen master to more deeply understand acceptance, how to put acceptance into practice, and ultimately how to teach it (Duckworth, 2015). Enter Dialectical Behavior Therapy, which doesn't focus exclusively on what needs to change; rather, it's a blended model featuring change *and* acceptance.

Interesting fact: Marsha herself wasn't a fan of the term "Borderline Personality Disorder", feeling that it was demeaning to suggest there's something wrong with *who you are*. I don't disagree and I believe this idea hit home for her personally, as she went public in a New York Times article in 2011 that she herself had struggled with Borderline Personality Disorder.

Given that individuals struggling with BPD suffer emotionally, she offered "Emotion Dysregulation Disorder" during a conversation in 2015 with the National Alliance of Mental Illness (Duckworth, 2015) as a more fitting label because it allows room for someone to be taught the proper skills for regulating emotions and alleviating their suffering. BPD symptoms don't have to be permanent!

Although this book is geared toward helping individuals struggling with Borderline Personality Disorder, DBT is helpful for a wide range of mental health issues and disorders: people who have problems with substance abuse, have suicidal thoughts or self-harm, have ADHD, an eating disorder, Bipolar Disorder, Anxiety Disorder, Major Depressive Disorder, or OCD (Moyer, 2021). So, if you don't have Borderline Personality Disorder, this book will serve not only as a tool for educating you about BPD, it can also help with whatever you personally are struggling with from a mental health standpoint.

## The Components of Formal DBT Therapy

This section describes the "standard" DBT model in case you'd like to pursue DBT under the guidance of a DBT-licensed professional. For now, these details are provided for informational purposes to give you an idea of what's typically involved.

Each therapy session and overall therapeutic setting is unique when it comes to the goals that are involved and the structure. However, certain characteristics of DBT do feature throughout, namely: group skills training, individual psychotherapy, and phone coaching (Schimelpfening, 2021).

Let's look at these in a little more detail:

- *Group therapy:* Behavioral skills are taught in groups.
- *Individual therapy:* Therapy sessions take place with a seasoned professional. You learn behavioral skills that are specifically designed to address the challenges you are currently facing in your life.
- *Phone coaching:* You are able to call your therapist between sessions whenever a difficult situation comes up so you can receive guidance on more effective coping strategies (Schimelpfening, 2021).

A lot more is involved in DBT than just learning basic life skills. In general, a series of steps are followed:

- *Stage 1:* When people turn to therapy it is quite common that they start off in a state of crisis. Therefore, it's important to help the person who is suffering from BPD to find stability, calm, and safety. It's the therapist's job to create such an atmosphere and it all begins by teaching the newcomer how they can gain control over their emotions.

- **Stage 2:** This is when the person who is suffering from BPD is able to stabilize their behavior, but can still act impulsively on the basis of their emotions. This causes trouble occasionally. Therefore, a mental health professional helps them investigate the causes of their emotional pain in a safe manner, instead of suppressing it.
- **Stage 3:** As time goes by, the focus shifts to maintaining the headway that has been made and to continue upholding healthy behavior. A reasonable amount of goal-setting is initiated, too.
- **Stage 4:** This part is more concerned with big-picture or long-term goals. The person in therapy gets to explore the goals that they want to achieve and look for ways to get the ball rolling. This stage is not only about finding happiness and stability, but is also concerned with achieving a sense of spiritual fulfillment (Eddins, 2021).

At this point, you might be wondering about the time frame. DBT takes about a year. However, the length of treatment ultimately depends on your specific goals, the nature and intensity of your diagnosis, and the type of program that you're involved in (i.e., whether it's an informal DBT program or a comprehensive one).

Comprehensive care means that you go for a year's worth

of individual therapy and participate in a DBT skills group for seven months. The group meeting usually takes place for 2-2.5 hours each week, and the individual therapy sessions usually take place for an hour each week (Eddins, 2021).

DBT itself is composed of four modules: Mindfulness, Distress Tolerance, Emotional Regulation, and Interpersonal Effectiveness (these will be discussed in depth in the chapters that follow). Typically, you spend 6 weeks on each module (Eddins, 2021). In general, the journey begins with individual therapy before you join a DBT skills group. When the skills group is complete, you will close off the whole treatment process by reverting back to individual therapy. Once again, this is usually completed within a year but can easily extend well beyond a year since everyone's progress trajectory is different.

That being said, you can choose to have ongoing, albeit reduced support after the treatment process is complete and continue with therapy for a longer period of time.

As for an informal DBT treatment program, the duration is shorter. Some of the reasons for this are that you don't have to participate in a DBT skills group and the nature of your goals might make it possible for you to engage in the process for a shorter amount of time.

Do take note that under normal circumstances, you can't participate in a DBT skills group without being in individual therapy. Who that therapist is, is up to you. They don't have to be part of the same clinic, or have any affiliation to the group.

What really differentiates DBT from other treatment options is the extended commitment that is required from the therapist and the person seeking treatment. Essentially, that's what makes it work and why it's so effective.

Here are some specific elements involved in the comprehensive treatment plan:

- *Acceptance and change:* During the therapy sessions, you will learn new strategies that can help you to be more tolerant of your emotions and life circumstances. Having a healthy dose of self-acceptance can sharpen the skills that you need in order to make a positive change in your interpersonal relationships and overall behavior.
- *Behavior:* Your therapist will help you analyze any destructive behavioral patterns that you might have so they can be replaced with ones that are healthier.
- *Cognition:* The main focus here is your beliefs and thought patterns. If they are not effective or helpful, the therapist will help you to change them.
- *Collaboration:* This involves teamwork and communication skills. Through DBT, you will learn how to communicate effectively. You have to rely on other people to help you, but in order for this to happen, you need to express your needs effectively. Typically, a therapist, group therapist, and psychiatrist, working together as a team, are involved in the process.
- *Skill sets:* You learn new strategies that can help you increase your skills.
- *Support:* Your therapist helps you look at your strengths and all the positive attributes that you have so that they can be developed and utilized to your benefit (Schimelpfening, 2021).

In the end, DBT can help you to express your emotions more effectively. You will start using coping strategies that can enhance the quality of your life.

Studies have shown that DBT works across a broad spectrum, including age, sex, sexual orientation, and race or ethnicity (Schimelpfening, 2021). Therefore, if you have worries about such factors getting in the way of your healing process, you can lay them to rest!

---

## Benefits of Reading this Book

If the previous section completely and utterly overwhelmed you, don't panic. It's a lot to take in, especially if this was the first time you're reading about Dialectical Behavior Therapy. The extensive commitment of the formal program is part of the reason this book was created. Many (or perhaps most?) people aren't able to engage in sessions of individual therapy and group therapy every week consistently for such a lengthy period of time. We have busy lives and competing priorities: jobs, families, elder care, medical issues, significant-others, life events and difficulties, not to mention the items that are listed below.

- ***Finances:*** When it comes to treating BPD (or any mental health condition), this can be quite financially taxing. Even though you might be covered by insurance, the options are limited and don't cover everything. These out-of-pocket expenses can add up and get quite expensive, especially if treatment lasts a year or more.

- *Availability:* Perhaps you might struggle to find a certified DBT professional in your area and, even if you do find one, there could be a long waiting list. This can make it hard to get into treatment even if you have the financial means.

- *Time commitments/limitations:* Going to therapy and group sessions over an extended period of time can be quite challenging. It is completely understandable that other life commitments could get in the way. That's why this book is so important in that you'll discover the essential skills that'll help you pursue your own healing. The best part is that it allows for self-pacing, so you can take it all in bite-sized chunks and customize the experience in a way that is appropriate for you. In short, you can cater it to your desired level of intensity and speed.

- *Jaded by experience:* Perhaps you've had a few DBT sessions before, or even just one, and you didn't have a good impression. In fact, DBT may have left a bad taste in your mouth. Maybe the therapist wasn't specifically trained in DBT or you didn't feel the therapist understood you; maybe you had some issues with the "contract", the "homework" that you had to do, or the "rules". Not to worry, this book puts all the power in your hands.

- *Credibility and streamlining of information:* There's a lot of information in various forms online, but when you start diving into DBT, it quickly becomes overwhelming and confusing. There are many bits and pieces that can be frustrating to sort through, figure out whether the source is credible, and make sense of potentially conflicting information that may surface. You eventually find yourself giving up and resort to watching videos of cats and dogs acting silly. This book brings all that content together in a way that is easy to digest.

Some of you may have started Dialectical Behavior Therapy but were unable to continue due to one of these reasons or something else. There are clearly a number of facets to a formal DBT program. This book steps in to offer you the chance you deserve for getting help. Doing the formal treatment program can give you the best prognosis for successful treatment, but if there are obstacles that prevent this from being a feasible option at this time, you can still experience benefits by giving yourself the opportunity for *self*-treatment.

This book is structured as follows: Chapter 1 takes a deeper dive into Borderline Personality Disorder, its subtypes and symptoms, and compares it to Bipolar Disorder. Chapter 2 will discuss Dialectical Behavior Therapy at greater length including an overview of the four modules and techniques. Chapter 3 will be about mindfulness as a way to manage intense emotions, and Chapter 4 will discuss distress tolerance. Chapter 5 will cover emotional regulation, which is what most people who have BPD struggle with. Interpersonal effectiveness is covered in Chapter 6 and alternative considerations for treatment for BPD are highlighted in Chapter 7.

The Table of Contents details the various skills of DBT so that, when you're having a difficult moment, you can quickly find the information you need and jump right to that section for immediate help. You may be looking at the TOC and wondering how you'll tackle this enormous beast, but fear not! You've got more willpower and perseverance than you might think. Don't look at the mountain; instead, look at the trail you're currently hiking and take it a step at a time. Before you know it, you'll find yourself on the mountain top enjoying the sense of accomplishment from how far you've come. You've got this.

# BORDERLINE PERSONALITY DISORDER

To provide a bit of perspective on what it's like to live with BPD, let's equate mood states to music. If a so-called neurotypical person experiences anger, sadness, or fear, the "volume" will be at a moderate level, like listening to a radio station. However, for someone with BPD, it feels like the sound or intensity of these emotions has been turned all the way up. It consumes them at full blast, as if they are standing directly in front of the speakers at a live concert.

Borderline Personality Disorder is much more common than most people think. Research has shown that, in the U.S. alone, about 1.6% of the population has BPD (Salters-Pedneault, 2020 [b]). So if you've been diagnosed with the disorder, you're definitely not alone!

At first glance, the number may seem quite small, but to put it into perspective, it means that there are more than *four million people* who have BPD - that doesn't seem so insignificant after all, right? In addition, BPD can often be misdiagnosed as an anxiety disorder or Bipolar Disorder. Therefore, the actual number of individuals suffering with BPD is truly unknown - it could be double, or even triple the number stated.

Whether you suffer from Borderline Personality Disorder and have a good understanding of how the disorder shows up for you, or if you know little about it, it would be useful to have a basic overview of its attributes.

Borderline Personality Disorder is a psychological condition that is highly complex and varies significantly from person to person in how it presents itself. BPD consists of unstable moods and emotions which, in turn, affect behavior (Salters-Pedneault, 2021). The instability translates into every facet of a person's life, whether professional or personal. It's among several personality disorders that are recognized by the APA/American Psychiatric Association (Salters-Pedneault, 2021).

The Diagnostic and Statistical Manual of Mental Disorders, 5th edition (or DSM-5) has a list of ten personality disorders that are divided into three sections, or clusters: A, B, and C. In Cluster A we have: Paranoid Personality Disorder, Schizoid Personality Disorder, and Schizotypal Personality Disorder. In Cluster B we have: Antisocial Personality Disorder, Borderline Personality Disorder, Histrionic Personality Disorder, and Narcissistic Personality Disorder. Finally, in Cluster C we have: Avoidant Personality Disorder, Dependent Personality Disorder, and Obsessive-Compulsive Personality Disorder (Gluck, 2021).

BPD can cause an incredible amount of distress. It has also been linked to numerous medical and psychiatric comorbidities, or co-occurring disorders (Chapman, Jamil, and Fleisher, 2022). For example, you may be diagnosed with BPD while, at the same time, have body dysmorphia (i.e., a mental health condition where you hyper-focus on certain perceived defects or flaws in your appearance even though they might not be real).

## Symptoms of BPD

The disorder can be diagnosed as early as age 12 but is most often diagnosed between late adolescence and early adulthood. That's not to say there aren't plenty of individuals who have been living with these symptoms for decades and have only now learned about the diagnosis (or still don't know for sure!). If the latter describes you, you may not have had an official diagnosis, but you'll likely recognize the symptoms discussed in this section. BPD is generally characterized by an unstable pattern of interpersonal relationships (including difficulties with rejection or being turned down), a distorted and poor self-image, and frequent outbursts due to difficulties managing or regulating your emotions. These symptoms are persistent and can be experienced quite regularly.

Let's take a look at the symptoms in more detail. However, do keep in mind that you don't have to have *all* the symptoms to be diagnosed with BPD. Also, the degree of intensity, when it comes to the symptoms, varies from person to person.

### *Deep fear of abandonment*

If you struggle with BPD, this point will not come as a surprise. Underneath the outbursts and unstable moods is a profound fear of abandonment. Strong efforts are made to avoid feeling abandoned, whether the fear is imagined or real.

You may need almost constant validation that the person isn't going to leave you, which makes it quite challenging to maintain healthy relationships.

### Unstable and intense relationships

You sway back and forth between two extremes: idealizing and then debasing the people who are close to you. Your relationships tend to be intense and characterized by regular bouts of conflict or arguments. You might find it difficult to trust others due to the aforementioned fear of abandonment, which puts a massive strain on your relationships.

### Disturbed and unstable self-identity

Issues with self-esteem and self-image/personal identity are pervasive. If you were raised in a chaotic, unsteady, even fearful environment, you derived your value and understanding of who you were based on how your caretakers reacted to you at any given moment. If their behavior was neglectful and highly unpredictable, you never had the opportunity to build a stable foundation of self.

### Chronic emptiness

You experience a persistent feeling of emptiness, or lack of purpose, and try to "fill up" this space with people, things, or actions. Some people may describe this feeling in other terms, like numbness, disconnection from self and others, general dissatisfaction, and apathy. This feeling can also manifest via thoughts such as "I don't fit in", "I don't like myself", or "I always feel alone" (Smith, 2020).

*Inappropriate emotional responses*

Another term for this is Mood Lability, which is characterized by a strong and changing emotional response to a situation, and it's disproportionate from the level of response that situation would call for. These responses can come on fast and furious and completely out of nowhere. Mood Lability shows up in other illnesses as well, such as PTSD and Bipolar Disorder. Often, these responses manifest in dramatic and intense bouts of anger which can lead to problems in relationships, both personal and at work (Salters-Pedneault [c]).

*Impulsivity*

You tend to behave impulsively or recklessly as you're seeking immediate relief or gratification in the moment, with disregard for consequences. This can take the form of shopping sprees, risky sexual behavior, substance abuse, binge eating/drinking, etc. There is also a high risk of engaging in self-harming behaviors, such as cutting or burning (which fall into the category of NSSI, or non-suicidal self-injury), and attempting suicide.

*Emotional instability*

This is a hallmark feature of the disorder. Changes in your mood occur rapidly, frequently, and unpredictably. They can last for a few minutes or hours, but don't generally go beyond a couple of days. You feel like you're on an emotional roller coaster. Mood shifts happen quickly in that you can go from feeling deep despair in the morning to feeling somewhat upbeat that same afternoon. Anger, anxiety, fear, and feeling overwhelmed are common emotions that tend to fluctuate as well.

### *Stress-related paranoid thoughts*

Another way to put this is: it's a fear of persecution. Thinking that others are out to get you, or are plotting against you. More specifically, when you feel stressed, you experience changes in your thought process, including paranoid thoughts (for example, thoughts that others may be trying to harm you), or dissociation (feeling spaced out, numb, or like you're not really in your own body). However, these thoughts normally go away once the stressor or trigger is removed (Salters-Pedneault, 2021).

## BPD Subtypes

There are four subtypes of BPD that are so varied it often contributes to misdiagnoses and may also cause a person with BPD to question their own condition when they compare their experiences to others and realize how much they differ. Although these subtypes aren't currently recognized in the DSM-5, there are abundant clinical cases and supporting evidence for these distinctions. That being said, an individual can have multiple subtypes or maybe have one subtype at an early stage of life and develop into another subtype at a later stage. Then there are some individuals who don't fit any of these molds (Pugle, 2022).

### Discouraged BPD (aka "Quiet" aka "High Functioning Internalizing")

This describes individuals who demonstrate neediness and reliance on others, and are generally pretty passive. However, when they are struck with a concern with abandonment, they can rage at themselves, experience deep despair, and have major difficulty tolerating feelings of distress. They can resort to self-harming behavior, have thoughts of suicide, and see themselves as terrible people. However, others may have no idea this person struggles deeply since they're so good at hiding their BPD and may even hold high-level positions of authority or management in their careers. People in this category can develop depression and/or anxiety. Misdiagnoses can happen when professionals seek to treat the depression or anxiety and miss the BPD because it's less evident (MedCircle, 2021). Other characteristics these individuals exhibit are perfectionism, self-isolation, seeking of approval, frequently feeling lonely/empty, neediness, and they may take extreme action to prevent abandonment, whether that abandonment is real or not (Pugle, 2022).

### Impulsive BPD (aka "Angry Externalizing")

For these individuals, rage can arise very quickly and can take others around them off-guard. There is very little tolerance for disappointment and distress but in opposition to

Discouraged BPD where individuals turn inward, they instead resort to expressing their extreme agitation by yelling, blaming, breaking things, etc. Impulsivity is common so these individuals might resort to drinking alcohol, doing drugs, and engaging in reckless behavior including attempts at suicide. These individuals feel completely overwhelmed and feel they cannot control the rage and strong emotions that arise. Sometimes this subtype can be misdiagnosed as mania due to the high level of externally-focused energy (MedCircle, 2021). They may engage in dangerous behaviors without any consideration for how it impacts others and the consequences that may arise. Other characteristics exhibited by people in this group are that they appear energetic, flirtatious, and charismatic. They may also be quick to get into physical altercations and engage in bingeing behavior (Pugle, 2022).

### Petulant BPD (aka "Histrionic")

This describes individuals who lash out at others when things don't go their way. They seek attention and don't have a high level of social maturity. Their focus is on things going according *their* expectations and can't tolerate the feelings of abandonment and stress that result from disappointment. The interesting aspect of this subtype is it can often overlap with symptoms of Narcissistic Personality Disorder as there are many similar characteristics. Note that this subtype shouldn't be confused with the separate Histrionic Personality Disorder, which doesn't include feelings of abandonment (MedCircle, 2021). Other characteristics exhibited by individuals in this subtype are that they seek control, or to manipulate others or a situation, they can quickly and dramatically flip moods, they're impatient and irritable, can be passive-aggressive, and perhaps defiant (Pugle, 2022).

### Self Destructive BPD (aka "Depressive Internalizing")

This describes individuals who exhibit such a pervasive and extreme depression that they have a very difficult time holding onto employment. It comes with very low energy, disinterest in making an effort, neglect toward themselves and even others in their care. The depression can deepen even further during triggering events such as disappointment, distress, and abandonment, which is what sets this subtype of BPD apart from Major Depressive Disorder (a common misdiagnosis) because the lows of the depression can be that much lower and more dangerous. These individuals have a high risk of harming themselves. Although this subtype has similarities to those of the Discouraged BPD subtype such as thoughts like "I deserve to die", "I don't know who I am", "I don't know why I exist", the emptiness and isolation experienced by this subtype is so debilitating it keeps them from being able to function in everyday life (MedCircle, 2021). Other characteristics of this subtype are that people may have deep feelings of self-hatred and/or bitterness, may feel a jolt in their energy level, a reduced need to sleep, and may jump into dangerous adrenaline-seeking activities without proper preparation. The latter three in particular can sometimes cause misdiagnosis of this subtype as Bipolar Disorder under the assumption the person is experiencing a manic episode (Pugle, 2022).

All in all, psychiatrists normally think of personality disorders as a persistent pattern of self-image or internal perception and external behavior (Salters-Pedneault, 2021). This means that you have a particular way of thinking about yourself and this extends to how you feel and interact with the world around you. Sometimes these two aspects are at odds when it comes to societal norms, and that's why it can interfere with daily life (Salters-Pedneault, 2021).

To recap, BPD and all the other personality disorders usually begin in adolescence or early adulthood, and continue to have an impact for many years. If no active steps are taken to treat the condition, it can cause a great deal of distress.

Once again, not everyone who has BPD experiences all the symptoms that were described. One person may have a few, while someone else may experience most of them. The condition itself is diagnosed by evaluating the symptoms on an individual basis and through a thorough examination of a person's medical history. Physical exams and lab tests are also performed to rule out any medical illness that might be contributing to the symptoms (Salters-Pedneault, 2021).

All in all, you need to experience at least five or more of the below symptoms in multiple contexts to be clinically diagnosed with BPD.

- Taking action to avoid abandonment
- Trouble with emotional stability
- Feeling empty
- Issues with identity
- Impulsivity
- Intense anger, disproportionate to the situation
- Problems with relationships

- Engaging in self-harm
- Experiencing paranoia or feelings of disconnection (Salters-Pedneault, 2021)

However, if you have BPD, the good news is that the right treatment can help you to live a happier, more fulfilling life.

---

## Contributing Factors to BPD

The root cause of BPD is still unknown, but what we do have is research that points to a combination of nature and nurture. Below are some of the factors that can contribute to your risk of having BPD.

### Brain structure

Research shows that there is a difference in brain structure and function in individuals with BPD (Salters-Pedneault, 2021). This is especially the case for the parts of the brain that are responsible for impulse control and emotional regulation. At this point, it is unclear if these differences have come about as a result of having BPD, or if they form part of the cause.

### Family history

If you have BPD in your family, this increases the risk that you will too. However, the home environment can play a significant role in reducing the risk. For example, if a parent successfully treated their BPD symptoms before having children, the parent won't demonstrate BPD behaviors when raising their children, which can lead to a more positive family dynamic.

### Negative experiences

Childhood abuse, trauma, or neglect are prevalent factors in people diagnosed with BPD. In many cases, the person was separated from their caregivers at an early age. As a caveat, not all people with BPD have experienced childhood abuse, trauma, or neglect and, conversely, a lot of people who have had these experiences do not go on to develop BPD (Salters-Pedneault, 2021). That's why it's important to keep in mind that a risk factor is not the same thing as a cause. If you've experienced certain risk factors, that doesn't automatically mean you will end up having BPD.

## Bipolar Disorder

People frequently confuse BPD with Bipolar Disorder (BD) because the nature of these two mental health conditions is so similar. In fact, some people are diagnosed with Bipolar Disorder when their symptoms better match BPD, or vice versa. In 2003 alone, studies showed that a whopping 40% were misdiagnosed with Bipolar II Disorder even though they met the diagnostic criteria for BPD, not for Bipolar Disorder (Ferguson, 2021).

On that note, let's take a deeper look into Bipolar Disorder. It was formerly known as Manic-Depressive Disease, and for good reason—just like in major depression, someone who has BD has depressive episodes. However, the two diverge when it comes to the point of mania.

When people experience Bipolar Disorder, they go through what are called manic episodes, characterized by periods of unusually high activity. They are very energetic and lively and this can last a while. They can't seem to sleep and their speech is quite fast. They may even take unnecessary risks, which includes gambling, overspending, or being sexually promiscuous.

In a period of mania, people will suffer from a delusion of grandeur, or an inflated sense of self. Some examples are believing they're a world-renowned celebrity, impervious to death, have mystical powers, can balance 50 plates on their head while juggling swords on a unicycle; you get the idea.

Hallucinations can also happen during a manic episode, and the person might experience a break from reality. In clinical circles, this is known as "psychosis" (Begum, 2021). However, given the rather negative association our society has with the word "psychosis", let's boil this down to people essentially seeing or hearing things that aren't actually there.

In addition, when they are manic, they may seek out pleasure, experience fast and scattered thoughts, high energy, and a lack of need for sleep. The pleasure-seeking can be especially dangerous because, when a person is experiencing mania, it can lead them to be extremely reckless. As a result, they can end up hurting themselves, or the people around them.

These unnecessary risks are taken because they have a sense of invincibility at that time. This feeling, however, is short-lived. When a manic episode inevitably comes to an end, a depressive episode takes its place, and there is a huge difference in character at this time. To others, the person may seem aloof, disinterested, and lethargic which is a complete 180-degree turn from who they appeared to be during their manic state.

On top of that, they may start to feel guilty for what happened during the manic episode while they were being reckless. For instance, they may experience buyer's remorse if they went on an epic shopping spree and now find themselves in debt because of it. Perhaps they started rearranging their living space and now find themselves in a huge mess of belongings or at minimum, unable to find the newly relocated pizza cutter.

Beverly Merz, the Executive Editor of Harvard Women's Health, sums it up as such: "In Bipolar Disorder, self-destructive behavior is usually followed by a period of depression" (2020).

Bipolar Disorder is classified under 4 main types:

- Bipolar Disorder I
- Bipolar Disorder II
- Cyclothymic Disorder
- "Unspecified" or "Other specified" Bipolar Disorder

The first type means the person has experienced one manic episode, at minimum, followed by a major depressive episode. Sometimes, the person experiences hypomania, instead of full-blown mania. Hypomania is more toned-down compared to mania. In addition, there is no risk of delusions of grandeur or hallucinations. In fact, hypomania may not interfere with any day-to-day tasks at all (Begum, 2021). The individual can function quite normally.

The episode, whether it's manic or hypomanic, usually lasts for about 7 days, while the depressive episode normally lasts for 14 days. Sometimes it can get so bad that the person may require medical assistance or hospitalization.

As for Bipolar Disorder II, this means that the individual would have experienced at least one major depressive episode, and at least one hypomanic episode. Mania does not feature in this particular disorder.

Cyclothymic Disorder is a completely different beast altogether. This has to do with the duration. Cycles of hypomania and depression generally last for at least two years. In addition, keep in mind that the depressive episode is not as intense when compared to major depression.

Most importantly, in children or teenagers, the cycle of hypomania and depression usually lasts for a year, not two years.

Last, but not least, we have "Unspecified," or "Other specified" Bipolar Disorder. It used to be called "Bipolar Disorder not otherwise specified" (Begum, 2021). This is when a person presents with a few of the symptoms of mania, or hypomania. This inevitably makes it hard to diagnose exactly which type of disorder it is.

The therapist may struggle to "fit" these symptoms into a common category. In fact, sometimes the symptoms don't last long enough to be considered an "episode" (Begum, 2021).

One characteristic that's experienced by some individuals who suffer from Bipolar Disorder is "rapid cycling". Rapid cycling is a term describing the duration/length of each shift between mania and depression. To be considered rapid cycling, an individual must experience a full cycle of mania or hypomania and depression at least four times a year (Begum, 2021).

Interestingly enough, research has shown that Bipolar Disorder (and rapid cycling in particular) is more prevalent among women (Begum, 2021). Rapid cycling can happen at any point in time and can disappear at any time. Most importantly, rapid cycling leans more toward depression than anything else, which increases the risk of self-harm or suicidal thoughts.

---

## BPD vs. BD

Even though there's some overlap between Bipolar Disorder and BPD (like changes in mood, impulsivity, low self-esteem or self-worth, and suicidal thoughts or actions), there are some significant differences, too. Let's take a look at them:

### *The timing of impulsive behaviors*

With Bipolar Disorder, impulsivity occurs during periods of mania or hypomania (once again, this is when an individual experiences a spike in energy, can't sleep, talks really fast, has an inflated sense of self, engages in harmful or self-destructive behaviors, and makes plans that they just can't seem to keep). However, in the case of BPD, the impulsive urges can strike at any moment. Mania is not involved. The urges are normally a response to stressors that happen randomly.

### *Sleep*

If you have Bipolar Disorder, whenever you experience a

manic episode, you feel more energized than usual and have a decreased need for sleep. BPD doesn't include manic episodes and sleep issues are generally not considered a primary symptom of BPD, but there is research that's starting to identify certain patterns of sleep irregularity that do occur for people suffering from BPD. Specifically, studies are showing that people with BPD have more fluctuation in their nightly sleep schedule than what's considered typical. These irregular sleep patterns can result in inadequate amount of sleep, lethargy, and trouble concentrating during waking hours. This type of fluctuation in sleep pattern is similar to people who suffer from Circadian Rhythm Disturbances (Moawad, 2022).

### Mood cycle time

Bipolar Disorder has mood cycles that shift between mania and depression, and they last for weeks or months on end. However, in the case of BPD, the mood cycles - albeit intense and frequent - are short-lived. They usually last a few hours or days. Someone with BPD can experience a sudden mood shift on the heels of something quite minor and it'll be extreme, such as going from feeling fine to battling feelings of devastation or desperation in a matter of seconds (Salters-Pedneault, 2020 [d]).

### Self-esteem

An inflated sense of self, known as "grandiosity" or "delusions of grandeur" in clinical circles, is a classic feature of Bipolar Disorder. This typically occurs within a manic episode.

The individual may even experience psychosis-like symptoms (i.e., delusions). This is absent from BPD.

### Relationships

Once again, a deep-seated fear of abandonment is a typical feature of BPD. If you have this condition, this means that you often struggle to have stable interpersonal relationships and are riddled with conflict. The conflict is a result of emotional outbursts that come from that very fear of abandonment. You may alternate between an extreme like and dislike for certain people. In the case of Bipolar Disorder, interpersonal relationships are no walk in the park, either, but a fear of abandonment isn't present under normal circumstances.

### Triggers

Suffering from BPD means that the way others treat you has a big impact on you, especially if you think someone is going to abandon/reject/leave you. Whether it's real or perceived, this fear of abandonment can trigger a major change in your mood state, which leads to conflict, self-destructive behaviors, or even self-harm. In the case of Bipolar Disorder, triggers can occasionally occur due to stress, or sometimes they can occur for no readily apparent reason (Ferguson, 2021).

## 2

# DIALECTICAL BEHAVIOR THERAPY

E ven though you're not responsible for having developed BPD, it is still important to be able to manage it. A specific idiom comes to mind - "playing the hand you're dealt". For those who haven't heard the expression, it's an analogy comparing life to a card game, like poker. Playing cards are dealt at the start of the game, and each player's hand differs in terms of the specific challenges they're presented with. You move through the card game (or life) and adapt your strategy accordingly.

Currently, DBT is the "gold standard" when it comes to treatment options for anyone who is struggling with Borderline Personality Disorder (Salters-Pedneault, 2020 [a]). In fact, studies have shown that 77% of people who underwent treatment for BPD by using DBT didn't present with the usual symptoms after a year (Salters-Pedneault, 2020 [a]).

Other studies have found that DBT is also effective in reducing hospital stays, the use of mind-altering substances, and self-harming behaviors (Salters-Pedneault, 2020 [a]).

Furthermore, it's an effective treatment method that's been known to reduce the risk of suicide (Schimelpfening, 2021).

Remember that, in most cases, BPD doesn't stand alone and some co-occurring conditions can feature in the overall state of a person's mental health. In fact, people with Borderline Personality Disorder have a high chance of being diagnosed with comorbid disorders. These include:

- Anxiety disorders 88%
- Mood disorders 80% to 96%
- Eating disorders 53%
- Somatoform disorders 10%
- Substance abuse 64%
- Attention deficit hyperactivity disorder (ADHD) 10%-30%
- Bipolar disorder 15% (Chapman, Jamil, and Fleisher, 2022).

Although DBT is most effective in its standard form with a therapist and group sessions, any number of the obstacles mentioned already in the "Benefits of Reading this Book" section can keep someone from engaging in the therapy formally and that's OK.

---

What Are Dialectics Anyway?

In the acronym DBT, the first letter stands for "Dialectical," but what does it actually mean? Dialectical is used to describe a situation where two opposing ideas can be true at the same time. By combining them together, a new truth, or way of looking at things can come to light. For example, you may sincerely believe that most people work hard and are doing the best they can, while still being convinced that they could do better.

Two people can experience the same thing very differently and both would be true; each person owns a part of the truth. A prime example is when one person says a glass is half empty and another says it's half full. Both are right and so is the third person who understands that the glass is *both* half empty *and* half full (Horne, 2021). This type of thinking opens the door not only for allowing yourself to feel conflicting things at the same time but to also acknowledge that another person's statement or observation (while being different from yours), could also be true.

Be aware of your inner monologue so you can create a middle way for yourself. The word "but" implicitly creates divisiveness so replace the word "but" with the word "and" as much as you can. For instance, instead of saying "I know I can do this, but it's not going to be easy," rather tell yourself "I know I can do this, and it's not going to be easy." Notice the feel of the statement changed when you swap "but" with "and". When you use "but", it introduces the feeling of an obstacle; however, using "and" allows you to accept that something's difficult and you're going to do it anyway. Psychologically, it ushers in a sense of possibility, optimism, and even power. Words really do matter.

Imagine if everyone thought dialectically? You'd hear rather open-minded statements like "I'm a Democrat and I see this Republican person has a valid point" or "My religion doesn't speak to that point and I'd like to hear more about yours". Clearly, this is not an easy thing to do, especially when it comes to divisive topics such as politics and religion, but imagine if we all made an effort to understand and accept one another even if we disagree with them. That would be revolutionary!

But let's start with something that will be helpful to you right now, especially if you engage in "splitting" behavior. Splitting is what happens when you look at yourself, others, or situations in extremes and there's no middle ground or gray area. An example is toggling between feelings that your friend is "the worst" when they disappoint you and "the best" when things go well. Another example is as you're returning home from a trip, you miss your exit and as a result, say to yourself "I'm a complete idiot! Why can't I do *anything* right?!" Of course you do things right! Making a minor error or oversight doesn't mean you *never* do anything right.

Splitting is a defense mechanism used in an attempt to try and protect the person from getting emotionally hurt, especially in relationships. It can either occur in cyclical episodes that last anywhere from days to years (Cirino, 2019) or it's a permanent state of mind, meaning that's how a person thinks all the time (i.e., right/wrong, good/evil, best/worst).

In summary, the term "dialectical" is meant to describe a situation where something unpleasant or conflicting is looked upon from a more objective standpoint. It aims to shed some light and create a deeper understanding of the present situation.

Things can always be perceived from more than one angle, even if those angles may seem contradictory. As mentioned earlier, two completely opposing viewpoints can still be true.

In the same vein, Dialectics aims to find balance by practicing radical self-acceptance while at the same time making space for personal growth and some much-needed change. By finding a good balance between two extremes, a new way of viewing any situation can be formed.

The "B" in DBT stands for "Behavior", meaning that you seek to understand and address a particular set of target behaviors. The frequency of these behaviors may need to be increased or decreased, depending on what would enhance the quality of your life. A common example would be a lack of self-care throughout your day-to-day routine.

The "T" in DBT stands for "Therapy". In a clinical setting, you'd be attending counseling sessions with a therapist but in the context of this book, this will be more along the lines of self-therapy.

The spectrum of coping strategies that individuals with BPD use in actuality aren't stress-relieving, but rather tend to make the situation worse and to push people away (thus, in effect, becoming a self-fulfilling prophecy). Seeking validation from external sources is a very common maladaptive coping mechanism that most people with BPD have. They seek it out in a manner that is almost addictive in nature (Krauss-Whitbourne, 2018). This can curb distress in the short term, but after a while, it becomes addictive and that's where the trouble starts. Think of it in this way: If you're constantly seeking reassurance in your relationships, it can be quite draining for the other person because they have to repeatedly reassure you to help you balance your emotional state.

As mentioned earlier, people with BPD have difficulty regulating their emotions and this easily leads to a situation where their relationships become quite unstable. They are normally filled with conflict. As a result, there is a high likelihood that they will resort to self-destructive behaviors (i.e., like binge eating or substance use) as a means of escape.

Self-harm is quite a complex issue and DBT aims to help anyone struggling with it to understand what contributes to the behavior and to help you manage the urge to engage in these behaviors. You also get to learn how to deal with painful emotions, reduce the intensity of these emotions, and improve your interpersonal relationships.

In Dialectical Behavior Therapy, you deconstruct what happens before and after a target behavior (Eddins, 2021), thereby preventing you from reacting in an extreme manner.

In this way, Dialectics aims to foster rational, logical, and objective thinking. You get to balance out the things that you need to accept versus the things that need to change. You get to consider things from the other side, and to put yourself in someone else's shoes. This is quite a powerful way to set yourself free from debilitating feelings or thoughts (Eddins, 2021).

DBT offers a roadmap that can help you handle intense emotions whenever they build up so that you can redirect them into something more positive, or at least less self-destructive.

With DBT, you shift your focus from the past to the present moment by asking questions like: "How can I handle this crisis now?" and " How can I cope right now?" (Eddins, 2021).

Instead of being distracted by the past, feeling guilty, or being judgmental, you learn to focus on problem-solving by looking for ways to improve your life from moment to moment. When your focus is on the present, there's no room for dwelling on the past or being riddled with shame about something that happened previously.

It was found that the frequency of suicidal thoughts

decreased drastically when those suffering with BPD learned how to manage and redirect their thought patterns (Eddins, 2021). This treatment plan has been used successfully for several decades, and today it is common knowledge that DBT is very beneficial for anyone who may not respond well to traditional modes of therapy or to medication (Eddins, 2021).

There is an exploration that takes place between self-acceptance and change in order to find a middle ground. You get to improve on your coping skills, and to find ways to manage your emotions. Most importantly, you also get to learn how to express them in a way that is effective, both for you and the people around you.

DBT promotes validation through acceptance. Acceptance in the context of DBT doesn't mean you approve or agree with what's happening, nor that you're ok with it. Instead, it's about non-interference. Let things be without trying to control them, or wish that things could be different. This can be quite challenging. Think of phobias for instance, like the fear of spiders. The mechanism of acceptance would urge you not to run away whenever you encounter a spider. This will feel uncomfortable - really uncomfortable in fact - and you'll probably be tempted to do just about anything to get away from it.

However, why not try something different? That's what DBT is all about—it promotes healthy coping strategies in times of stress, or when you're feeling some intense emotions. Allow the experience to unfold, and take a deep breath. Stay a little longer, even if it's just an extra second, before the urge to flee overtakes you. Next time you might go up to two seconds, then three. Before you know it, spiders won't bother you as much!

Acceptance, or the capacity to allow something to happen

without interfering, requires practice and small steps to be taken consistently, but the effort is well worth it! It means that there is nothing overpowering you, or inhibiting the quality of your life. You get to step into the world with a sense of freedom and tranquility.

---

Techniques of DBT

Let's take a look at the main DBT techniques that are used for distress tolerance. These will be detailed further in Chapter 4.

- *TIPP*
- *ACCEPTS*
- *IMPROVE*
- *STOP*
- *RESISTT*
- Self-Soothing
- Pros and Cons
- Distraction

Three goals that you work on with respect to distress are:

- Accepting distress
- Finding meaning in your distress
- Tolerating distress (Eddins, 2021)

The main aim is to accept a situation as it is without making spur-of-the-moment judgments. Another way to look at this is you're acknowledging a situation that is happening or has happened and hitting the pause button before you get swept up into a tornado of suffering due to having made premature conclusions about the situation.

Try using a keyword or key phrase in mind that you use to remind yourself to pause before automatically making conclusive judgments about a situation, like "OK", or "Yep, that's what happened". Maybe even count to 5 in your head or snap your fingers to remind yourself to halt judgment - whatever works! This is important because accepting reality puts you in a position of empowerment as you begin to make better choices rather than dwelling on the moment or being anxious about the future.

Radical acceptance is a huge part of the healing process in DBT. It urges you to face the fact that a lot of things are out of your control. This can be easy to forget when you are feeling deeply upset about something. Instead, you might end up ruminating as certain negative thoughts replay themselves in your mind. You might think of a certain situation as being unfair, and wonder what you've done to deserve it.

Unfortunately, such a position is not empowering, but defeatist. However, radical acceptance can help you to think about any situation in a healthier way, or in a more positive light. You learn to accept things just as they are and not waste time thinking about how they could be different. This lessens anxiety, depression, and feelings of anger.

Not only do you get to accept the situation for what it is, but you also make an earnest attempt to find meaning in it. For example, instead of feeling frustrated that you're stuck in a traffic jam and resorting to road rage, radical acceptance could nudge you to look at things differently. The time could be used wisely and seen as a blessing in disguise. You could listen to a podcast, queue up your favorite song and sing along out loud, or call a friend and catch up. The thought is: This traffic jam isn't what I wanted or was looking forward to, but maybe it's a sign that I need to slow down and to focus on something else. At the very least, I can choose to do something more enjoyable in this moment instead of rage at the near-infinite line of cars ahead of me.

One point to stress is that acceptance doesn't mean you become a doormat. If you're in an unhealthy relationship, for example, "accepting" someone belittling you constantly is not one of those times you go with the flow. You always want to be looking out for your wellbeing, and being in an abusive relationship does not serve you. In keeping with the theme of acceptance, my advice on that subject is to *accept* that that relationship has served its purpose, you've learned some valuable lessons along the way, and it's time to move on.

---

## Core DBT Skills

### *Mindfulness*

DBT increases self-awareness. In other words, your mindfulness skills have a chance to develop. Mindfulness means that you are living in the present moment. There is an active attempt to pay attention to what is happening around you and inside you. You explore your thoughts, feelings, and even your physical body (i.e., you become aware of your facial expressions, body language, heart rate, breathing, etc.) by engaging your senses. This way, you learn to tune in to what's happening all around you from a more detached stance (i.e., while not being so judgmental or critical). These skills can help anyone, including you, to slow down and stay calm. This, in turn, opens up the space for more effective coping skills, especially when your emotions are running high. In this way, it becomes easier to avoid responding to certain situations in a manner that is automatic and unthoughtful. In other words, you're less likely to resort to your default, which, in this case, is negative thought patterns and impulsive behavior.

### Tolerance

During therapy sessions, you will be equipped with distress tolerance skills. This makes it easier to accept any situation as it occurs. Some of the techniques for handling a crisis include: distracting yourself, self-soothing, and being aware of the outcome of not tolerating distress (Schimelpfening, 2021). In short, these techniques prepare you for the times when your emotions may run high, or when they may be quite intense. The goal is to empower you so you can handle them in a more positive way over the long run.

### Social Effectiveness

This pertains to your ability to navigate the interpersonal relationships that you have. The main purpose of social effectiveness is for you to be more assertive in expressing your needs. The skills you learn enable you to say "no", while still managing the relationship in a positive and healthy way.

### Communication Skills

These skills are paramount to have, especially the ability to listen actively. Communication skills make it easier to deal with challenging people, and to have a good level of respect for yourself and the people around you.

### Emotion Regulation

This can help you deal with overwhelming feelings in a manner that is more effective. The skills you learn in DBT will challenge you to identify, name, and change your emotions. Once you come to grips with your negative emotions (e.g., anger, frustration, etc.) and are more able to cope with them, your emotional instability and vulnerability will be reduced. As a result of this, you'll be able to have more positive emotional experiences. One key tactic to achieve this goal is called "opposite action". Recognize how you're feeling and do the exact opposite (Salters-Pedneault, 2020 [a]). For instance, if you're used to withdrawing from your family and friends when you feel down, make plans to see them instead!

## Potential Challenges

In conclusion, if you're someone who wants to "own" your own treatment, on your own time, without the potential hazards of judgment or social engagement, keep reading. Please take to heart, however, that DBT - both in the formal clinical setting as well as this self-paced book - is not a quick and easy solution. It involves time, practice, more practice, and commitment to wanting to make this work for you.

Anticipating that there could be many pitfalls along the

way helps you set expectations before you jump on in. That way, when the ride gets a bit bumpy or you find yourself veering off course, you won't blame yourself because you'll know that's an expected part of the journey.

Given the length of DBT in its formal clinical setting, remember to please be kind to yourself when you're trying to go it alone. You're not expected to learn and polish these skills in the blink of an eye. Far from it. You've been using maladaptive coping skills your whole life and it's very hard to break lifelong habits immediately. Take this opportunity now to promise yourself you won't give up. And if you need a little extra support or encouragement along the way, there are Facebook groups you can join where people are similarly working through their BPD symptoms using DBT skills.

That being said, DBT isn't a universal cure-all. Although there is abundant evidence in support of this treatment's efficacy and many individuals with BPD have claimed that DBT has changed their lives, solutions that help 100% of people are few and far between. You may even find individuals who say that DBT doesn't work, but what likely failed them is their therapist or how the program unfolded for them specifically. This isn't meant to discourage you, but rather to help you understand that you are NEVER to blame, ever, for DBT "not working". Read that again: You are not at fault if DBT has failed you in the past or if it doesn't provide you with at least some symptom relief if you've put in the work.

Your motivation to improve your life, even a little bit, is what will keep you going. The potential reward of a more satisfying (and less distressing) existence is worth the effort. With that in mind, let's dive in.

# 3

---

## MINDFULNESS

Mindfulness is a core skill when it comes to Dialectical Behavior Therapy. It involves paying attention - without judgment - to how you're feeling in the moment. It is done consciously, and the aim is to look at things from a more detached stance, or in a more objective light.

This can be quite a difficult thing to do considering the current pace of life. Such a chaotic external environment can be stress-inducing and, as a result, it can be hard to gain a sense of peace. This is especially the case if you're struggling with BPD, because you're more prone to being emotionally reactive.

So as you're going about life, going to work, studying, taking care of the kids, pets, and trying to juggle a myriad of other things, how is it possible to curb judgment and attachment? How can you remain neutral in the face of failure or major accomplishments? The answer is: mindfulness.

Research has shown that mindfulness reduces stress and can help anyone to feel at peace (Greenwald, 2020). There is an unfortunate myth that it takes a lot of time to practice mindfulness, that you have to dedicate a ton of hours for it to work. This is not true. You can practice it for any length of time, as long as it suits your needs. It could even be just 5 minutes if that's all you have. Any little attempt can have massive benefits (Greenwald, 2020). That being said, practicing mindfulness on a regular basis (i.e., being consistent) is crucial and it can decrease your stress levels drastically.

Another myth is that mindfulness has to be done at a certain location, like sitting elegantly atop an expensive cushion in the quietest corner of your beautifully furnished, clutter-free home, or atop a picturesque waterfall while dappled light from the forest canopy shines lovingly down upon you. Well, it sounds nice but is terribly impractical, and is certainly not a requirement. You can be mindful anywhere, even during your restroom break at work - take any opportunity!

And on that note, let's take a look at the different ways that you can begin to implement mindfulness into your daily routine.

------

## HOW and WHAT Skills

The "How and What" skills are great for practicing mindfulness and, as a result, can help you to have a better handle on your emotions. Practicing these skills will help you to be able to think and act from a more balanced place. DBT emphasizes finding a place of balance that involves both your Rational mind and your Emotional mind. If you imagine your Rational mind sitting on one end of a see-saw and the Emotional mind on the other, in the middle at the balance point is what DBT refers to as Wise Mind. It's the "middle way" where you are using both minds to identify what action or decision is in your best interest.

Wise Mind also introduces the concept of using your intuition, or "gut feeling". In fact, a quick way to access Wise Mind is to ask yourself "What do I know in the depths of my soul/being to be absolutely true?" (Gatewell Therapy Center, 2020). Wise Mind is a space where you feel balanced and have a sense of clarity and control; practicing mindfulness is an effective way to get there. When you're in this headspace, you're aware of both your Rational and Emotional minds but neither of them is controlling you (Gatewell Therapy Center, 2020).

If you're unable to have Wise Mind present during a particular event or conversation, you can still access it later. After enough time has passed, you have the opportunity to reflect on the incident and achieve greater clarity and insight than you did in the moment.

Now, on to the *How* and *What* skills you can practice to help you develop mindfulness.

**WHAT:**

- *Observe:* Notice your thoughts and feelings.
  Become aware of your internal or mental state, and external or physical state. Most importantly, let the experience just happen, don't try to suppress it.

- ***Describe:*** This part is about naming how you feel. As you begin to observe your emotions, try to label them. For example, "I feel frustrated. My jaw is clenched and my chest is tight."
- ***Participate:*** Be present. Engage fully in what is happening, even if it means you have to experience some difficult things. These moments are all necessary (Sunrisertc, 2017).

**HOW:**

- ***Don't Judge:*** As you begin to observe, avoid making any snap judgments. Just notice what is going on on the inside and outside. This is not the time to make any evaluations, particularly ones that split things into "good" or "bad." If this happens, just replace it with something more descriptive.
- ***Stay Focused:*** Direct your attention to what is happening now, so you don't get distracted with thoughts about the past or future.
- ***Do What Works:*** As you begin to observe what is happening in the moment, make sure that whatever you decide to do next is helpful in the short and long term. In other words, your actions must reflect what is most effective to do in that moment or in your current situation (Sunrisertc, 2017).

---

### Mindful Eating

When you're doing something as habitual as eating, chances are high that you zone out and don't even notice what you're doing or what's happening around you. So the next time you're whipping up a meal in the kitchen, try to be mindful. Be fully aware of what you're doing as you eat or as you're preparing your meal. Enjoy all the sensations, from the way the food tastes and smells to hearing something sizzle on the stove. Notice the texture, the size, the scent, and pay attention to how it feels as you put a little of it into your mouth. This can make a habitual thing that you do on a daily basis a completely new experience. True story: I once closed my eyes and put a raisin in my mouth slowly, took time to observe its texture, size, and sweetness, and when I finally bit into it (very deliberately) the first time, I felt an explosion of taste in my mouth. As I chewed it slowly and mindfully, it was the best raisin I ever had! There was nothing special or magical about that particular raisin - the savory flavor was the result of the way I mindfully ate it that resulted in the experience.

Chopping carrots or lettuce can be a way to center yourself as you listen to the crunch of these vegetables while they're being cut. Focus on the sound as the blade cuts through them, and pay attention to the force that it takes to do the task. You can even focus on the size of the chunks, and so on. Many people do these things quite absent-mindedly while they think of everything else they have to do after they're done eating. But that stuff isn't going anywhere. Do yourself the favor of focusing all your attention on the task at hand. It's ok when you lose focus and are distracted by something. Just make sure to come back to that place of focus.

### Mindful Walking

The next time you go for a walk outside, don't put headphones on or completely lose yourself in your thoughts. As your feet touch the ground, pay attention to how it feels. Be aware of the sounds and smells around you. My personal favorite is jasmine, getting to walk past them each summer when they're in bloom is such a treat. I always pick a stray flower or two on my way back so I can keep smelling them long after my walk is done.

These days, whenever I smell jasmine, my mind automatically goes back to the relaxing walks that I have on a regular basis. A positive association has been created with the scent (i.e., a pleasant, peaceful walk). Therefore, if I'm stressed out, all I have to do is smell jasmine and I instantly feel calmer. I even carry a small bottle of the scent with me in my bag.

If you can engage in something similar, this can be a great way to cool off and to let go of any thoughts, feelings, or emotions that are not serving you. Be conscious of every step that you take while you're on your walk. You could even play a game, like avoiding any cracks on the pavement (or making a conscious attempt to step on them). You could also count the steps between two objects or more, like the lamp posts, fire hydrants, or mailboxes.

### Writing with Your Non-Dominant Hand

Think of some encouraging phrases or affirmations and

then write them out 10 times with your non-dominant hand. Probably you're going to feel frustrated, or start to judge yourself because you're used to having a certain level of mastery and control. This is the perfect opportunity for you to practice releasing these feelings. Engage fully with what you're doing, notice the extra level of concentration that you need if your writing is going to be legible.

### Listening to your favorite song/album

We all have that one album or song that we return to. Maybe you first heard it on a road trip that you took as a child, or on a date with a special someone. Listen to the music with your full attention. Pay attention to the words and lyrics. What message is the artist trying to convey? Also take note of the different instruments. What can you hear? Is it just the piano? The guitar, drums, or the vocals? What other sounds might you have missed before? It's quite shocking to realize how many sounds might have been missed even though you've listened to the song countless times before.

### People-Watching

Whether you're sitting on a park bench, having a quick snack at the food court at your local shopping mall, or simply looking out of your window, observe the people around you. Not to say you have to turn into a creep, but just notice what is going on around you. Watching people in action can really help you to look at things from a more detached stance. Perhaps consider wearing dark sunglasses to help you "hide" so people don't know you're watching them. Or at least it's harder to tell!

Personally, having the experience of just watching people in action prompted some existential questions to pop up for me. You realize how many things people get distracted by that are not that important. That being said, refrain from making any judgments. Just slip in and out of the experience like an ocean wave that ebbs and flows.


### *Practicing Compassion*

Choose a comfortable spot in which to sit or lie down, then focus on your breathing. As you do this, repeat the following phrase: "I am at peace, I am happy." Once you've really started to concentrate on this mantra, switch your focus to another entity—it could be a person, a pet or animal, or a plant. Repeat the same mantra, but just change the name: "May you experience peace and happiness." Remember to be aware of your breathing as you say this mantra (Greenwald, 2020).

You may be feeling the furthest thing from peaceful or happy, but just saying these mantras repeatedly shifts something in your brain. It's the same idea as forcing a big smile even when you don't feel like it. It automatically lifts your mood, relaxes the muscles in your face, and gives the signal to your brain to feel a little less stressed.


### *Making Tea or Coffee Mindfully*

Make some tea or coffee for yourself, or serve some to a guest. Take your time and be aware of your movements. Be as detail-oriented as possible. For instance, notice as you lift the pot by its handle with your hand, and hear the sound of boiling water pouring into the cup. Notice the fragrance as it wafts into the air around you. Each step is done in full awareness. Once again, take note of your breathing as you perform this task. In fact, try to breathe a little more deeply than usual. This can help to slow you down. It is also a great way to keep focused if your mind strays.

### Washing the Dishes Mindfully

Pick up each dish and treat it as if it's sacred. Feel the warm, bubbly water between your fingers and the steam on your face as it rises up to meet you. Be conscious as you begin to wash each dish individually. Treat each piece of cutlery or crockery as an object of contemplation (Schultz [b], 2020). Be mindful of your breathing if your mind starts to wander, and don't try to rush through the entire process. Consider it to be the most important thing that you could possibly be doing at that moment. You can also do this if you have a dishwasher; I typically will rinse plates before stacking them and you can do the same, but not absent-mindedly. Do the same as above, though instead of getting the plate 100% clean, your focus is on slowly rinsing each piece as you hold it, turn it in your hands, glide your hand across the surface, reach for the dishwasher, etc.

### Cleaning the House Mindfully

Divide the work up to make it more manageable, from putting away books, clothes, or toys, to scrubbing the bathroom and sweeping the floor. Give yourself enough time to complete each task. Move consciously and unhurriedly. Give each individual task your full attention. Don't forget your breathing, especially when your thoughts start to take over.

For example, as you're putting away your books or magazines, feel their weight in your hands. As you start to place them on the shelf, look at what you're holding. Be aware of the texture and title. Don't make any abrupt or harsh movements.

Don't just focus on the big picture of "cleaning up," but instead, keep your mind on each small task, whether you have to mop the floor or put each of your kids' toys away in a special bin. Being so methodical may seem pointless and something you don't want to do since it'll slow you down, but the benefits are worth it. Reframing a task to its simplest definition and focusing on just that instead of thinking about the next thing you have to do can allow your mind to slow its frantic pace. And at the end of the task, you're rewarded with the added bonus that the area is now clean!

### Bathing Mindfully

Give yourself a chance not to rush through this very important process. Take a bath for at least 30 minutes. From beginning to end, be slow and methodical in each action. As you start the process, take note of how you are preparing the bath water, and as you finish off, be fully immersed in how you are slipping on some clean clothes. Be aware of every single part of your beautiful body. Any judgments, discrimination, or fear should be left outside the door. By the time you're done, your mind and body will feel light. The simple act of bathing can be a spiritual experience and help you to feel at ease if you let it. Include scented candles, incense, aromatherapy oils, bath salts, bubbles, soothing music, and even some wine, if you wish.

### Connecting to the world around you

It is possible to find a sense of peace and calm no matter what you're doing, even if you're just sitting on the sofa, for instance. Start by focusing on where your body touches another inanimate object. It could be the ground, the floor, the bed sheet, or even your clothes. Feel how connected you are to what is around you. These objects are accepting you into their warm embrace, just as you are, all the time.

Think about the function of that object and how it relates to you. In other words, look at all the ways that it is serving your needs. Feel the texture of the fabric on your couch for instance, let it run through the palms of your hands, and look closely at the patterns on it. Focus your attention on being connected to it. This couch, at this very moment, is taking care of you, showing you love, showing you kindness. It has accepted you in totality. It is holding you up, supporting you, and stopping you from falling to the ground. Let these feelings enter your heart during such a simple act. You can practice the same technique at any time or place, with almost anything.

A classic example is the ground. It is holding you up, and carving an infinite path of possibilities for you so you can choose where you want to go. Quite literally, it's not letting you down. You don't have to be afraid of being sucked into a deep, dark abyss.

The walls in your room, or around your house, can also be used to sharpen your mindfulness skills. They keep out harsh winds, the rain, the heat and the cold. They also keep you

42

warm and safe at night. Most importantly, they give you privacy and keep out the ones who you don't want to be there. These walls give you a place where you can be yourself.

## Breathing Mindfully

The point about being conscious of your breath was brought up a number of times throughout this chapter, and not without cause. It is the first and easiest way to start grounding yourself in the present moment.

Before we get into specific exercises, I want to take a few moments on a detail that is all too often overlooked: *how* to breathe deeply. If I told you to take a deep breath right now (go for it), take notice of what happened in your body. Most likely your shoulders rose and your chest expanded. This "chest breathing" is how most of us breathe throughout the day (perhaps with the exception of trained monks and meditators). This is actually a shallow means of breathing and we're not breathing into the full depths of our lungs.

If you breathe in a shallow manner, it activates a sense of panic and increases your cortisol levels (i.e., it will trigger your parasympathetic response, or fight/flight response). So the next time you feel anxious, notice your breathing. Most likely it will be on the faster side and shallow. The reason why is you're not getting enough oxygen. Therefore, if you counteract this by breathing deeply through your abdomen, you'll be able to calm down (Schultz, 2020 [a]).

The same applies to deliberate breathing during some breathing exercises (note there are breathing exercises where you're not taking deep breaths, you're just being aware of your normal breathing). We want to induce a sense of peacefulness and the way to do this is to fill your belly with your in-breath first, and once it's completely full, keep breathing in and then you'll notice your chest starts to expand. Now THAT is a deep breath.

With this instruction in mind, let's take a look at some techniques that you can use to practice breathing in a mindful manner.

One very effective technique is to practice breathing deeply and slowly while envisioning colors as you do so. Pick one color that represents your inhalation and another that represents your exhalation. You can choose the colors for any reason. Maybe red can be the exhale because it represents the feeling of frustration that you want to let out while the color blue represents the calm, cool feelings that you want to enter your body. Close your eyes and alternate these colors as you focus on your breathing (Greenwald, 2020). Imagine and try to "feel" the color permeating into your lungs on the in breath and transforming into the other color as the breath exits your lungs.

In his book, Peace is Every Step, the Buddhist monk, Thich Nhat Hanh. gives some really effective breathing techniques, too. They make life a little calmer and enjoyable. This particular exercise uses simple words, or a mantra. As you inhale, tell yourself: "I am breathing in" and as you exhale, tell yourself: "I am breathing out." That's it. Recognize the breath that you are taking in and the breath that you are releasing. You don't even need to say the whole thing, you can choose to only use two words: "In" and "Out" (Schultz, 2020 [a]).

The reason for saying these two phrases or words is to reduce your focus to the single task at hand. This is all about simplifying the moment, to collapse your mind from an enormous fireball of scattered and intense noise to a single neutral act that reduces you to your simplest level of being. You exist. Focusing on your breathing is proof of your existence, and probably the most fundamental statement of reality that there is: "I am".

This technique can keep you focused on the moment and, as a result, your breathing will be steady and peaceful. Your mind and body will also be at ease. It's not really a hard thing to do and the best part is that you can reap the benefits in just a few minutes. Most importantly, using such a breathing exercise can create synchronicity between your mind and your body.

A lot of the time while people are busy with life, their minds drift off and they start to think of one thing, while their bodies are doing something entirely different. This creates a mismatch between these two aspects of their being.

However, you can avoid this mismatch by being conscious of your breathing and heart rate. You can unify these two aspects so they can become whole again. Like a bridge that connects one land mass to another, conscious breathing connects your mind to your body. As Thich Nhat Hanh says: "When we breathe consciously, we recover ourselves completely and encounter life in the present moment" (Schultz, 2020 [a]).

It's important that you take long, deep breaths through your nose and not your mouth, because this helps to slow down your heart rate and breathing. As you're breathing, place one hand on your chest and the other on your stomach and breathe in deeply. Make sure it's deep enough that you can see and feel your stomach rise as you breathe (Hanh, 1992). Once you perform several of these deep breaths, you will feel your mental state start to shift.

You can use breathing techniques any time you want to feel more relaxed, or when you need to bring yourself into a completely different headspace that is much calmer. That being said, the aim is to be more accepting of reality, not to fight against the tide.

You can enhance the experience by listening to podcasts on meditation, or you could even implement some physical activity, like going for a walk.

If you find a sense of panic arising as you try to breathe in deeply, reverse the sequence and see if it helps. In other words, breathe out first and then breathe in. It may sound like a ridiculous suggestion, but sometimes small things make a big difference.

Find a comfortable spot where you can sit or lie down. Put your arms at your sides, and your palms facing up, towards the ceiling. Close your eyes. Begin to breathe slowly through your nose. Observe how the in-breath fills up your body, how your abdomen and chest work together so your lungs can take in life-giving oxygen and sustain your existence in this moment. With the out-breath, you've transformed that oxygen into fuel for plants and trees. You can even picture your out-breath making a beautiful flower grow and blossom. You can do this exercise anywhere, even during your lunch break at work. It doesn't need to be done lying down, you can even do it in an upright position while sitting at a desk.

If you have the inclination, check in with yourself during your breathing exercises to see if there any points of tension in your body. Does your chest feel tight? Is your jaw clenched? If so, deliberately relax those areas and focus your breathing into those problem spots.

These simple DBT breathing exercises can keep you anchored in the present moment. They can also reduce stress and depressive thoughts that you might be struggling with.

Don't worry about getting it completely right the first few times. It's not about being perfect. Mindfulness is a technique that is meant to sharpen your awareness. Remember to be kind to yourself as you practice it.

Of course, mindfulness is not a magic pill that is going to solve all your problems. Inevitably, life is going to be stressful at times. However, being mindful and compassionate can make difficult situations feel more manageable.

# 4

---

## DISTRESS TOLERANCE

W hether it's something big (like losing your job), or small (like stubbing your toe), there are going to be times when you don't have control over certain events that happen in your life. It is at moments like this that you'll need a high level of distress tolerance. Like a rubber band, it can give you the ability to snap back into form.

You'll need this skill if you're going to make it through tough situations without falling into despair, or engaging in unhealthy coping mechanisms (i.e., smoking, binge eating, drinking copious amounts of alcohol, etc.). These so-called coping mechanisms act as a means of escape from your mental and emotional state. But remember, emotions will come and go. Using DBT can help you to overcome these difficult moments with more grace and ease.

---

The first technique for distress tolerance that is going to be discussed is called "IMPROVE." It will help you handle any intense emotions until they start to subside. The acronym "IMPROVE" stands for: Imagery, Meaning, Prayer, Relaxation, One thing in the moment, Vacation, and Encouragement. Let's take a look at each one in detail.

---

*IMPROVE - to make the moment more tolerable*

### Imagery

This involves visualizing yourself dealing successfully with any problem. Imagine the feeling of accomplishment that will wash over you the moment it's done. By doing this, you just might be able to change the outcome of whatever is in the way and overcome it.

### Meaning

Even though it might be hard at first, especially when everything is still fresh and emotions are running high, try to find meaning in any undesirable situation. What can be learned or gained from it? Perhaps you have lost some people in your inner circle who aren't meant to be there, and you now have the opportunity to find new ones, or maybe the experience has taught you to be more patient, empathetic, etc. It is always possible to find a reason for your suffering.

## *Prayer*

Don't be afraid to tap into your spiritual side. Find a form of prayer or meditation that works for you. You could address a higher power, whether it's God, your own "higher self", your spiritual guides, or the universe directly. Practicing the art of total surrender can help you tolerate any situation a little more. You can also choose to carry an inspirational quote that's especially powerful for you if the word "prayer" doesn't resonate. The goal is the same - tap into something greater than yourself that uplifts you.

## *Relaxation*

When people feel stressed, they tense up physically. It has to do with their built-in fight or flight response. However, by engaging in certain activities, you can feel calmer and ease any psychological distress that you might be feeling. You could practice deep breathing, take a hot shower, go for a relaxing walk, or do some yoga which reduces stress and promotes mental health.

Try hip-opening stretches to increase your balance and flexibility. In yoga circles, hips are referred to as the body's emotional junk drawer. The reason for this is that this part of the body is the seat of self-expression and creativity. It is also the wellspring of sexual energy and passion. Most notably, the muscles around this area actually store strong negative emotions, like anger, fear, anxiety, worry, and grief. So by practicing hip openers, your body will get to release these emotions (Burgin, 2022). Should you feel some strong emotions while you're in that pose, take a step back and observe them. Be mindful of what is going on inside you and ask yourself: "What is this emotion trying to tell me about myself?", "How does it make me feel?"

### One thing in the moment

When you feel stressed, try and focus on the present moment and let go of the past. Don't hyperfocus on the future, either. Ruminating on issues that have come and gone, or worrying about the potential consequences of a situation that is out of your control (or hasn't even happened yet) will not aid in the resolution of said situation. Find an activity that can help you keep your mind on the present moment and dedicate your entire being to that task. It could be anything, from picking up a coloring book, working on a puzzle, or exercising at your local gym. Focusing on one thing can help you to feel less overwhelmed.

### Vacation

Needless to say, going on vacation is a blast. Is it always practical? Absolutely not. But you can do a brief "staycation" where you commit to doing only things that serve you in some way. Get your hair or nails done. Prop a beach chair outside to get some Vitamin D on a sunny day. Treat yourself to a nice footpath with Epsom salts. Go to a yoga class. Read something you enjoy. Find any way you can to break away from all the things that usually cause a lot of stress. If you're really strapped for time and resources, take an imaginary vacation. You're on a beach at a fancy resort, getting an amazing massage, listening to the ocean (if you can find some ocean sounds to supplement this imaginary vacation, even better!).

Include as much detail as you can, like the warm sea breeze, birds singing, the sound of palm leaves rustling in the breeze. If you put a lot of sensory imagery into your "design", it can become a powerful place you can quickly return to when you need to calm yourself down.

### *Encouragement*

You don't necessarily need external validation, or for someone to give you encouragement for it to be effective. In short, it doesn't have to come from the outside. You can give yourself encouragement by using certain mantras like, "I've got this", "I can do it", or you can even borrow the famous line from Luca: "Silencio Bruno!" (which is telling your emotions to quiet down). Say it loud, and say it with conviction! You just might be surprised at how quickly you're able to motivate yourself whenever you're having a hard time (Dietz, 2017).

The next technique is called "STOP" - let's take a closer look at what it means:

*STOP - to pull you back from the edge*

- *Stop:* Remain calm and be still. Resist the urge to react to something in the moment by being in control of your thoughts and your body.
- *Take a Step Back:* Try not to act on impulse. Get yourself away from the situation if possible and concentrate on your breathing.

- *Observe*: Disengage from your thoughts. Look at your surroundings instead, and explore how you're feeling.
- *Proceed Mindfully*: Keep your goals at the forefront of your mind. Consider the ways you can achieve them under the circumstances (Eddins, 2021).

---

## Self-Soothe

Self-soothing is about getting yourself to calm down without relying on anyone else. In DBT, it is recommended that you do so by engaging all five senses. The aim is to reduce any impulse to react to negative emotions. For example, you could use all five senses when going for a walk outside. Look at the trees, and the sky above. Listen to the birds singing. Ground yourself by feeling the grass between your toes. Smell some flowers. You could even tickle your taste buds by taking a small snack with you along the way. That being said, let's take a look at the 5 senses individually.

### Sight

Focus your vision on something else. If you're in a room, for instance, focus on the colors and textures. You could even pull out your phone and scroll through some pictures that you really like. Maybe hone in on a specific part of the photo that you haven't really noticed before.

### Hearing

Listen to the sounds around you. Are the birds chirping outside, or can you hear the sound of traffic? I used to live by a busy road with constant traffic, which I converted in my mind to the sound of a waterfall (they sound remarkably similar!) and enjoyed it more that way. You could even crank up the volume on your favorite song if you want to. Alternatively, there are many apps that you can install on your phone if you're looking for soothing sounds.

### Taste

A small, tasty treat can be a wonderful thing. It can take your mind off whatever you're thinking and usher in a pleasurable experience. If you're in a rush, or not in the mood, don't worry. It doesn't need to be a whole meal, a simple piece of gum or a few breath mints can work, too. If you can find the willpower, grab a small piece of chocolate and pop it in your mouth but don't chow down right away. Let it sit and melt and savor it for as long as possible.

### Touch

This can be experienced in numerous ways. You can run your fingers through your hair, play with a fidget spinner or any of a vast number of tactile toys out there - squeeze balls/gadgets, goo, kinetic sand, or if you have a pet with soft fur, that's always a personal favorite. Warm baths and snuggling up under a blanket count too! So does pulling weeds (in my personal opinion, anyway); there's something gratifying about grabbing hold of a clump of crabgrass impinging on your beautiful flower bed and seeing if you can pull it straight out, roots and all.

### *Smell*

Focus on the aromas in the air. Can you identify any of them? Are some cookies baking in the oven? Or maybe you can smell some coffee brewing in the office kitchen? One of my favorite smells is wood burning from someone's chimney or fire pit. There's something warm, comforting and even nostalgic about it, especially if your area is blanketed in snow. If nothing interesting exists for you naturally, create your own: put a few drops of your favorite essential oil into a diffuser, or light some incense. These scents can be very calming (Sunrisertc, 2017).

---

## Pros and Cons

When you feel like acting on impulse, consider the pros and cons of doing so. Write them down.

Then write a second list, but this time consider the pros and cons of NOT giving into your impulses. Try to keep this list with you at all times, you can even transfer it to your phone (Eddins, 2021). That way, when you start to feel overwhelmed or distressed, you can review it and remind yourself why it's important not to act out.

Making a sensible decision can be quite a hard thing to do, especially when you're not in the right frame of mind. However, using a pro and con list to weigh out the consequences can help to put things in perspective. When you are in an emotional crisis it can stop you from acting on impulse. The list doesn't have to be very comprehensive. It can be as simple as a few bullet points.

All in all, this is a very useful tip because it can help you choose better alternatives and avoid any impulsive urges or their negative consequences.

---

## Distraction

Negative thoughts, feelings, and emotions fluctuate. They come as easily as they go. Therefore, it could be worth just taking a breath and letting them pass. Having some distractions to bide the time can make it a whole lot easier. "ACCEPTS" is an effective way to distract yourself, so let's take a closer look at this technique.

---

## ACCEPTS - to distract yourself

In DBT, the acronym ACCEPTS is used as a reminder to keep yourself busy when you feel distressed. The acronym stands for:

### Activities requiring thought and concentration

This can be any activity that stimulates you, on either a mental or physical level. You can read a book, call a friend, work on a brain teaser, or even meditate. The options are endless. If the activity only manages to hold your attention for a short time, you can always move on to a new one. (You never know, by the end you just might have a very productive day!).

### Contributing to something meaningful

Think about what you can do for the people around you in their time of need. Being kind or being of service to someone else can be a good break from any heavy emotion that you might be experiencing. It can relieve you of emotional distress and help get your mind off things. Helping others can also make you feel good about yourself. The world is your oyster and you can really choose just about anything, from washing the dishes when it's meant to be your partner's turn, to helping your neighbor get dinner on the table. These activities can be a great distraction from your current situation.

### Comparing your situation to something worse

This is about looking at your problems from a more objective standpoint. Has there been a time when you've had to face a challenge that is more difficult than the one you're facing right now? What did you do? Maybe this is the most intense situation that you've ever come across and you're feeling really stressed about it. In that case, you might need to look outward. Is there another person who has suffered more than you have? Are you safe in your house, while someone else doesn't have that luxury because they're in a war zone, or they lost everything because of a natural disaster? The purpose of this exercise is not to add more fuel to the fire, or to make you feel more stressed than you already are, but it's simply a way to broaden your horizons.

### Evoking a competing emotion

You are more than capable of invoking the opposite emotion whenever you're feeling stressed. Practice a bit of mindfulness, watch some adorable YouTube videos of kittens, or Google search "adorable puppies". Put on lively music. Dance! All in all, switching things around by invoking the opposite emotion can help to decrease the intensity of any negative thoughts or feelings.

### Pushing the emotions from your mind

If you feel overwhelmed and can't deal with something in the moment, it's completely okay to set it aside for another time after you've had a chance to collect yourself. You can push the problem out of your mind temporarily by (envisioning yourself) stuffing the emotion into a cardboard box, sealing it with tape, and putting it up high on a bookshelf. Tell yourself you'll deal with it later. If that emotion leads to an urge to self-harm, grab your phone and set a timer for 60 minutes and delay any action until that timer is up. If at that point you're still feeling the urge to self-harm, time to reset the timer!

### Thoughts first, save emotions for later

You can replace negative thoughts and feelings with activities that can keep your mind occupied, like doing a Mah Jong or Sudoku puzzle. Most importantly, these distractions can prevent a situation where you resort to unhealthy coping mechanisms due to the negative feelings that you might be experiencing. It's a way to give yourself some time to cool down until you can naturally regulate your emotions.

### _Safe sensations created to distract emotions_

Hold an ice cube in your hand. Take a cool shower or otherwise dunk your face in cold water. Got an onion or a lemon handy? Cut a small piece off and lick it. Hot sauce or Sriracha? Put a dab on your finger and lick that. As discussed in the section on self-soothing, you can use your senses (safely) to distract yourself from emotional suffering. Prepare a delicious meal if that works for you but please don't blast eardrum-piercing music through your earbuds (that would be _un_safe!).

---

### TIPP - to change body chemistry

The tips that are coming next are another means to help you deal with emotional turbulence. The idea behind most of these skills is not to "remove" or completely eradicate distress from your life. You will experience upset, discomfort, torment, and pain. But what can you do so it doesn't completely overtake you?

Let's take a look at a technique called "TIPP." You can use it when you feel like your emotions are about to bubble over, or when you're not able to process information properly because those emotions feel like they're about to take the wheel and drive. It's also useful if you're experiencing extreme hardships for the first time. TIPP stands for:

### Temperature

Try to decrease your heart rate by regulating your temperature. You can do this by using something cold, like holding ice cubes in your hand, letting the car's AC blow on your face, or splashing some cold water on your face. Are you warm and cozy but it's freezing outside? Stick your head out there. When we feel angry or agitated, our bodies often heat up. However, this technique can quite literally cool you down and counteract this effect.

### Intense exercise

This is the opposite of what was outlined above. You have to increase your heart rate for a bit (about 10-15 minutes). The main objective is to switch up your physiological reaction to how you're feeling and to distract you. You can jump rope, do jumping jacks, ride a bike, swim a few laps in the pool, or run on a treadmill. You don't need to be a marathon runner, you can match the form of exercise to your preferred level of intensity. Increased oxygen levels in your body can help you to feel less stressed, and the best part is that it's hard to stay mad when you're exhausted.

### Paced breathing

Paced breathing is a breathing technique that is also known as "box breathing." You'll be counting to four repeatedly for each of these steps: (1) Count to four while breathing in (2) Count to four while holding your in-breath (3) Count to four while exhaling and (4) Count to four while your lungs remain empty. Repeat. This can help you to feel calmer when you're feeling emotionally triggered. Do this for a few minutes. Breath control can have a profound effect on your mood and emotional state because it counteracts your body's fight or flight response.

## _Progressive muscle relaxation

This part is less focused on your breathing and more focused on your body. The point is to contract/tighten each muscle group for five seconds and to follow that up by loosening them. This can help you relax. Focus on all the muscles in your body, one at a time, from head to toe. When we tighten our muscles voluntarily and then relax them, these muscles become more relaxed than before. The most fascinating thing is that relaxed muscles need less oxygen, so our breathing and heart rates naturally slow down. In short, as your muscles relax, you'll begin to relax mentally, too. (Sunrisertc, 2017).

---

## RESISTT - to deal with overwhelming emotions

RESISTT is a combination of 7 techniques that can help you have a better handle on your emotions whenever you might be feeling overwhelmed.

### Reframe the Situation

When something appears to be inescapable, it's quite common for our minds to switch to black-and-white modes of thinking: "I'll never be able to get rid of all my debt" or "I'll never get out of my depression". Reframing means that you look at things from a different perspective. It's about finding an alternative story to tell yourself. For example, instead of telling yourself the story that you're doomed to be depressed forever, you might think "I've had good days and bad days - this is just a particularly bad day so things seem extra gloomy" or "I'll be able to release my depression once I find the right tool. It's out there and I just haven't found it yet" or "I'm feeling depressed and my goal is going to try and have more good days than bad days to the best of my ability". Even if you're feeling depressed 97% of the time, there's still 3% of the time that you are out of that depressive state so you *know* it's possible.

Try to find objective arguments and look for points where things might not be as bad as they seem. In no way does this invalidate how you feel or what you're going through; the main goal is to help you look at things from a more realistic standpoint.

### Engage in a Distraction

Have a list of activities that are pleasurable to you. Then pick one that can really keep you engaged mentally and/or physically. This will help to take your mind off the current situation.

Simply telling yourself to stop thinking about something isn't the way to go. Most likely, it will just make you think about it even more. It's the exact same scenario as when you're told not to think about blue flamingos. What's the first thing that you end up doing? Probably thinking about blue flamingos.

### Serve Someone Else

Instead of focusing on your emotions, problems, or any unhealthy coping mechanisms that you might have, you can shift your attention to someone else. Perhaps you can help a friend out by babysitting for them so they can take some time off, or you could volunteer at your local animal shelter, or you could surprise your partner by making their favorite meal. It doesn't even need to be anything big. For example, you could simply take some time to listen to a colleague's story without judgment.

If you have the financial means, you can make someone's day by leaving an extra large tip for the kind waitstaff at a restaurant or pay for the meal of the person behind you at the fast food restaurant's drive-through. Challenge yourself to try something like this just to see how it makes you feel. Even if you never get to experience a "thank you" from the person since you walk out of the restaurant or drive off, rest assured you absolutely-100%-without-a-doubt *know* that you put a smile on someone's face. Knowing that you wield that kind of power might actually put a smile on your face.

Take a moment to think about some interesting ways you can help the people around you (even if they're complete strangers), and make a list. That way, you can always turn to it when the need arises.

### Invite Intense Sensations

Whenever you're going through some painful or difficult emotions, it can be quite helpful to divert your attention away from them by filling up your senses with something else. These sensations are very intense, but not harmful in any way. For instance, take a cold or hot shower, go into the sauna, jump straight into a pool or ocean, take a walk in the rain for a bit (not long enough to get a cold, though), or sit outside in the hot sun for a bit. If you're insanely ticklish, that's another option for you! The main point is to experience these intense sensations in a way that is safe.

### Shut it Out

If you're feeling stressed, anxious or overwhelmed, a change in environment can do a world of wonders. If possible, go to a place where you know you will feel relaxed and calm. This will anchor you to the present moment and help you to be more mindful.

If you do this, but still find yourself struggling to let go of how you're feeling, or struggling to let go of a particular situation, ask yourself whether you'll be able to fix the problem in the present moment. If you are able to solve the problem right now, then do so, if not, then write it down on a piece of paper, crumple it up with force (that way, you're symbolically "compacting" the problem) and leave it somewhere for you to rediscover later.

If you still can't let go of whatever is bothering you, draw an imaginary line on the floor with your foot. Then take an exaggerated step over that line, telling yourself you're leaving that thing behind and stepping into a new state of being of your choosing. You can do this with any boundary or edge - from carpets to hardwood, a doorway threshold, or step across a large crack in the sidewalk. Basically, you can use whatever line or border supports your being able to move yourself physically, and thereby mentally, from "here" to "there". From one state of being to another. "I'm leaving my disappointed state behind and stepping into a calm state". Put an exclamation point on this action by taking a deep breath and exhale as you cross the line to make it even more real for you.

### _Tackle and Neutralize Negative Thoughts_

This is meant to encapsulate anything that doesn't add or contribute to your feelings of distress. For example, you can count to ten or practice your breathing (as was described in Chapter 3 when we talked about mindfulness).

You could also take a step back and just soak in what's around you. Notice your environment and the objects in it, their colors, textures, smells, and sounds.

Another useful strategy is to think about your favorite song. Go ahead and sing it! Belt out those tunes to your heart's delight. You're bound to feel better afterwards, especially if you throw caution to the wind and don't care how you sound. Sing off-key - who cares? Play with the melody a bit and transform the song into your own custom version.

Another way to stop yourself from thinking in black and white terms, so that your thoughts are more neutral, is to repeat a catch phrase that is helpful to you. For example, "It is what it is," "Never a failure, always a lesson," or "Never, ever give up."

### Take a Break

What it means to take a break is different for everybody. Perhaps you can put off some work or chores for tomorrow if it is inconsequential. If you can take a day off work, then do so. It can be useful if it's done sporadically (Olson, 2018 [a]). Of course, you wouldn't want to do this on a regular basis because it can create a situation where you postpone so many things for so long that a backlog ensues.

This, in turn, will just become another problem that you need to deal with.

Let's consider how this technique can play out in a stressful situation. Perhaps a friend of yours starts to make some comments about your outfit one evening while you're out. This, quite understandably, makes you feel embarrassed and judged. You feel yourself spiraling and get the urge to smoke even though you've been trying to quit and have successfully gone cold turkey for the past three months.

However, this situation is emotionally charged for you and you're almost sure you're about to relapse. In fact, you feel like you could chain-smoke a whole pack of cigarettes.

To overcome this situation, *start by reframing it.* Perhaps initially, you were under the impression that your friend was mocking you or being spiteful and this made you want to rage faster than the Hulk. In this case, you would take a step back and maybe consider the possibility that you're sensitive towards this particular issue because deep down you're insecure about your appearance. If your friend knew how you felt, they'd apologize and tell you that they weren't trying to be mean.

Afterwards, you could *engage in a distracting activity.* To cool off, you decide to treat yourself to some chocolate chip ice cream and a leisurely stroll on the beach.

When you get home, you call up a very good friend of yours and catch up for a while. You find out that he needs some help picking out a wedding ring because he's decided to propose to his long-time partner. You're thrilled at the prospect and the both of you go shopping! (i.e., *Serving someone else.*)

After you're done hunting for a ring, you feel the need to open up to your friend about what happened earlier, to just get it off your chest. While you're doing that, he invites you to take a walk with him in the cold weather for a while (i.e, *inviting intense sensations*). This really helps you to clear your head.

When you return home, you decide to take some time away from the friend who made you feel some intense emotions. It is a more constructive approach than getting extremely angry at her or arguing with her. That being said, do take the time to explain to her that you need some time for yourself (i.e., *shut it out*).

While you're taking some time to yourself, you make an effort to *tackle and neutralize any negative thoughts* by not resorting to black-and-white modes of thinking. You know this happens when you feel hurt or rejected, so you concentrate on thoughts that are more neutral, like: "I acknowledge how this situation made me feel. It's interesting that I reacted that way."

In the end, you decide to *take a break* from your usual routine, and this (plus the previous steps) prevents you from chain-smoking.

# 5

## EMOTIONAL REGULATION

A person's communication with themselves is typically known as their "self-talk," "internal dialogue," or "inner monologue." It is a cognitive and neurological activity. People tend to engage in it more often when they're faced with obstacles or feeling stressed. It can be external, meaning that they can vocalize their thoughts, or internal, meaning that it is silent.

Self-talk can also be positive or negative. However, in this day and age, it tends to lean toward the negative. For instance, social media, pressure from other people, and pressure on yourself, can make your self-talk highly critical.

Positive self-talk, on the other hand, is an inner monologue that has a favorable outlook on who you are. It gives you the warm and fuzzies about yourself. It's also a great way to think optimistically and get motivated.

In short, positive self-talk keeps people going when the chips are down, and helps them to look on the bright side. Examples of positive self-talk include: "I am really proud of myself," "I have personal power," "I am perfectly me," and "It's not ideal, but it could be worse." These can also be used as affirmations, or mantras.

Positive self-talk has many benefits, especially on a mental level. For instance, one study conducted in 2020 (in Iran) showed that self-talk had an impact on how people were able to cope with anxiety during the COVID-19 pandemic. Those who engaged in positive self-talk had lower levels of anxiety and fewer symptoms of Obsessive-Compulsive Disorder (Richards, 2022). The reason for this is that they were able to come up with effective strategies to handle their emotions and mental stress.

Even in the case of athletes or individuals who are passionate about sports, positive self-talk has been shown to motivate them and improve their performance (Richards, 2022). In fact, a study conducted in 2020 found that positive self-talk also helps athletes to stay engaged and have fun during practice or competitions (Richards, 2022).

With all this in mind, the main objective of the upcoming section is to give you some tips on managing your emotions and ways that you can boost your levels of positive self-talk. This is really important if you're struggling with BPD because of how easily your moods fluctuate. One moment you're feeling good and you have a positive self-image, then the next moment things change drastically and you can't even look in the mirror.

Our thoughts can be productive. They have the ability to usher in a sense of joy and peace into our lives, or they can be quite destructive. Unfortunately, because of the pressure that people feel from the outside, they become highly self-critical. Examples of negative self-talk look like this: "I'm not good enough," "I ruin everything I touch," "I'm a failure," or "I'm a burden to my family, friends, partner, etc".

These thoughts normally begin to take root from a very young age. Most likely they are a result of what was said to the person, the type of treatment they received, and the experiences and expectations that they had (Richards, 2022).

These thoughts have a massive influence on people and are quite difficult to overcome because they were repeated frequently, perhaps even on a daily basis, for many years. After an extended amount of time, negative self-talk became a way of life and perceived as the truth. Given the amount of time it took to construct this permanently negative perception of yourself, it follows logically that it's not going to change overnight. This is something you chip away at by practicing awareness of when that negative self-talk is happening. It's so engrained in us that it's second nature and we most often don't even realize it's happening.

The subconscious is a very powerful thing. It can manifest and bring to life the ideas that people have of themselves. If you continue to let your brain get away with telling you you're an awful person and you don't deserve to live without challenging the idea, unfortunately you are reinforcing that reality for yourself every single time you have that thought. Consider the example of coming down with a bad cold. You start telling yourself and others how sick you are. If you keep repeating "I'm so sick, I'm so sick, I'm so sick", guess how you're going to feel.

In other words, your thoughts can become a self-fulfilling prophecy. So when good things happen, you might consciously, or unconsciously, sabotage them just to prove to yourself that you were right. Once things don't work out, which inevitably happens because you brought about the result, these instances are used to further validate the perception that you have of yourself. Consequently, the negative thoughts that you have of yourself get reinforced (Sullivan, 2018).

As an example, let's suppose you connected with someone online and you're going on a first date with them. Before the date, you've already built up thoughts such as "I'm going to ruin this, just like every other date I've gone on" or even something more subtle like "This isn't going to go well".

On your way to your date's location, you're asking yourself why you're still single after all these years and have to be going out on pointless dates when your friends are happily married with kids. You never seem to fit in and there's no one out there for you. When someone finds out *who you really are*, they're not going to want to deal with your issues. You've got too much baggage. Every past relationship has ended in catastrophic failure, why should this be any different? Why even bother? This is going to be a waste of time.

You arrive at your date and you're feeling anything but cheerful given all your thoughts leading up to this moment. Maybe you should just turn around and walk away to avoid having to deal with yet another failure - you just can't take it. But before you get a chance, your date mentions your name and you look up. You sit down for a coffee but don't feel terribly conversational (thanks to the less-than-wonderful things you've been telling yourself). Maybe by now you've made a snide remark or two at your date or mentioned something about how gloomy the weather is. After all, what difference does it make since this is going to end in failure anyway? You might as well say what you want, throw out some boundaries, and enjoy a free coffee and danish.

After your date ends, a couple potential scenarios can arise. You never hear from them again or they text you saying something along the lines of thank you, but you're not a good match. Both of these situations lead to feelings of failure and maybe you feel disgusted at yourself. Maybe you're angry at yet another let-down. And oh by the way, you say to yourself "ah HA, I knew this wasn't going to work out!".

Can you see though, how every thought leading up to the date and during the date set you up for failure? It's not *who you are* that's the problem, it's the persistent loop of negative thoughts running on auto-pilot in your mind that beat you down. You may feel like "so what, that's the real me", but it's not. You are not your thoughts, but your thoughts have an enormous influence on who you *think* you are. If you could change those thoughts, or at least challenge the validity of them, could things be different? Is it worth trying in the event it actually works and discover that the "real you" isn't what you thought?

At this point, you may be wondering how corny it is that you need to talk yourself up and how fake it feels, like you're lying to yourself. Don't worry, I'll offer two suggestions.

The first is to engage in positive thinking by following the steps below, the most important of which is bolded at the top of the list. Regardless of whether you continue through the remaining bullet points below or take my second forthcoming suggestion, it's critical you engage in this first bullet point either way.

- **Investigate and break apart any negative thoughts that you might have, then challenge them. Make sure to take note of any examples where they are not true.**
- Reframe these thoughts into something positive.
- Repeat positive thoughts about yourself on a daily basis. For instance, you can say some positive affirmations in the morning and in the evening because that is when our defenses are down. We are more susceptible to the power of suggestion at these times (i.e., when we are close to waking up or falling asleep). That being said, you don't have to set any limits, you can even say them to yourself all day long (Sullivan, 2018).

Here are some examples of the first bullet point, of how you can challenge negative thoughts.

You think: "I suck at everything".
Challenge: "No, I don't. I'm a great dog-mom. I can cook like anyone's business. I'm great at axe-throwing competitions. I can roll my tongue and cross my eyes." Get creative here. You definitely do NOT suck at everything.

You think: "Things can't get any worse".

Challenge: "Oh yes, they can. I could have limited faculties (seeing/hearing/mobility). I could be living under a bridge. I could be starving because I can't afford food. I could be seriously ill with no cure in sight. A hurricane/tornado/earthquake could take everything I love away from me." Note: My sincere apologies to anyone who has gone through any of the aforementioned; the key is that no one goes through ALL of these events and there will *always* be something that could be worse.


You think: "I'm hopeless"

Challenge: "No, I'm not. I'm hopeful because I know there's something out there that will help me - I just haven't found it yet. I'm breathing. I have great ideas. I'm awake and have use of my mental and physical faculties. I have a mind and it serves me well in many ways. I have a sibling/parent/aunt/uncle/child who loves me for me. I have a support group that believes in me. I can do anything I put my mind to".


Now for my second suggestion, which is get an inspirational deck that speaks to you. I've found that pulling a card and reading it to myself strikes a deep chord and uplifts me into a better, kinder headspace. There's a vast range of card decks available online, but I think that Kate Allan's Thera-pets: 64 Emotional Support Animal Cards (Self-Esteem, Affirmations, Help with Anxiety, Worry and Stress) is probably the most relatable to the majority of people. You'll see from the over 1,800 reviews on Amazon that people love these cards so much they even frame them for permanent display around their homes!

In summary, any thoughts that you have, whether they are negative or positive, can become powerful if you pour your time and attention into them. The message is clear: You can choose to grow flowers, or weeds, in the garden of your mind. Therefore, if you want to be able to regulate your emotions with more success, start by consciously directing your thoughts toward the positive.

Choose where you want to put your attention, time, and energy. Initially, it might be quite hard to make a change, especially if you've been operating in a self-deprecating manner for quite a while. In such a case, positive thoughts might not come as naturally or automatically to you. However, with time and practice, it will become easier. Put differently, this frame of mind will be more accessible to you.

---

## Opposite Action

When we feel a distressing emotion, we tend to behave in accordance with that emotion. For example, if you're feeling really low or depressed, you may feel lethargic. You may just want to shut the world out and ball up under a blanket on your couch all day. With depression, there's typically little interest in doing anything at all; what you feel like doing is absolutely nothing and so that's basically what you end up doing. The issue with this is that by lying around, you're not actively doing anything to make yourself feel better. Instead, you're effectively reinforcing how you feel and probably making yourself feel worse. This can end up in a hopeless loop of feeling bad, acting in accordance with feeling bad, then continuing to feel bad (or worse) (Self-Help Toons, 2020).

The idea of Opposite Action is to do something completely different from how our feelings want us to act. So, instead of doing nothing when you feel depressed, do something. Anything! Go outside and sit on the stairs or a bench - anywhere that isn't your couch and where you can get some fresh air. That's a start and it breaks the vicious cycle of reinforcing your misery. Essentially, by changing the things we do, we can change how we feel.

Let's look at another example - anxiety. When you feel anxious, you want to withdraw from the thing or situation that is making you anxious. However, continuing to avoid what causes these feelings to arise will continue to make that anxiety real for you (Self-Help Toons, 2020). This applies to fear as well; people avoid what they fear but does that help the fear of that particular thing dissipate? Absolutely not. The only way to make the fear dissipate is - you've got it - you face the fear. Usually, when we approach something we fear and decide to push through it, or at least make baby steps towards eventually pushing through it, it lessens the severity of that fear and you gain confidence that you can overcome. So, in the same vein as facing your fears, face your anxiety, and stay there with the triggering thing or situation. The longer you can stand the exposure to the anxiety-inducing trigger, the more your anxiety will lessen next time you're faced with a similar trigger. You're basically convincing yourself it's not as bad as you made it out to be.

Finally, let's take a look at how to apply opposite action to anger. When you're feeling angry, you probably want to counterstrike, to fight back, but that can lead to more trouble. Not only will you then have to deal with the consequences of acting on that anger with the thing or person you took it out on, but you'll also likely keep stewing about the situation, replaying it over and over in your head and probably end up making the anger more intense. Acting on anger certainly won't lead to feeling better about yourself. If you choose to do something completely different instead, say you take a mindful couple of breaths or even drop into your favorite yoga position, the anger should come down a notch or two.

When you're angry, you're in a very narrow, focused state of existence like a bomb that's ready to explode at the slightest touch. Compare this to the feeling of joy, if you've experienced it, or seen in a child. A child in a state of joy is open; there's a sense of spaciousness, like the world is the child's oyster. This is very different from the way a child who is timid, perhaps even afraid, acts. They may be found hiding in a corner and feeling like the walls are closing in. Anger feels similar, like you're in a vise that's tightening around you, so the suggestion is to create spaciousness by perhaps envisioning yourself high above your body observing yourself and the thing that's triggering your anger. By expanding your awareness and increasing the perceived amount of "space" you have in a situation, you'll likely be able to reduce the intensity of the emotion. From 100 feet up, does that situation look as intense as it does at ground level?

*ABC - for self-care*

One very effective technique in DBT that helps people to regulate their emotions is called "ABC." This stands for "Accumulate positive experiences," "Build mastery," and "Cope ahead."

You'll be able to find a bunch of new hobbies and talents, and this technique can also teach you some very useful skills that you will need in order to overcome difficult experiences. Let's take a look at each point in more detail below.

### Accumulate Positive Experiences

It is important to make more deposits than withdrawals in the bank account of life. This is meant to relay the message that your life will go well and you will have a better perception of it if you have more positive experiences than negative ones.

If your life is going to be balanced, you need to put more into it than you take out of it. Research has shown that people can bounce back quicker from a setback if they have a high number of positive experiences.

However, if you have a large number of negative experiences (even if they are just *perceived* to be negative but might not necessarily be so), then any tiny issue can feel really overwhelming. It's that typical scenario where you accidentally spilled some coffee on your shirt on your way to work, came late due to traffic, and the rest of the day just seems to take a nose dive from there. By the time you return home, any minor incident can seem catastrophic.

However, this situation can easily be avoided if you build up a reserve of positive emotions by doing something that uplifts you on a regular basis. Once you've accumulated some positive experiences, it will be easier to overcome sadness, anxiety, or stress when you're going through a tough time because there are so many positive memories that you can look back on. They can remind you that life can be bright and cheerful, and help you to move forward.

These positive experiences can be split into two: Short-term and long-term positive experiences.

A short-term positive experience is something you find pleasurable that you can do on a regular basis. It's quick, easy, and fun.

Gardening, playing board games with the family, going camping with friends. These are the types of activities that we do occasionally, so their effects don't stick around for too long. Doing something regularly, at least one thing every day, can be a great way to build your resilience. You will be able to overcome negative emotions more easily. That is why people who meditate do it every day - you need to set yourself up for a good day every day. People who exercise every day notice they don't feel the same if they skip a day. To put it another way, yesterday's coffee isn't going to help you wake up today; you drink that cup of coffee *every* day for the results you seek.

That being said, do be aware of your state of mind while you're busy with the activity. Are you physically present, while your mind seems to be wandering elsewhere? You don't want to miss these moments—that defeats the whole purpose. Enjoying an experience means being mindful of it. So if you start to notice that your attention is elsewhere, refocus on the activity at hand. Later on, that "in the zone" feeling will become a habit and you won't get distracted as much.

If you're looking to do something that is high in energy, you can go for a run, clean the house, play with some animals or pets, go for a drive, go rock climbing or hiking, scour different parts of the city, or spend time on an excursion with the kids.

However, if you're keen on something that is not so energy-consuming, you can watch a movie, do arts and crafts, journal, call a friend, look through old photos, read a book, do some yoga, download some apps, go out to lunch, get a facial, get your nails done, or bake some cookies or muffins that you can donate for a good cause.

As for long-term positive experiences, these are very powerful and meaningful. They can help you to build a life that is full of purpose and meaning.

Think of them as milestones. It could be graduating from high school, going to college, traveling, landing your dream job, getting married, or having a family. It all depends on what you value in life.

If you're not sure how you can identify your long-term goals, or how you can begin to craft long-term experiences, here are a few tips:

- Make a list of your top values. What is important to you? What do you hope to achieve out of this life? Once you identify what you value in life, you'll have a clearer pathway to action. You'll be able to think of ways that you can uphold these values. Afterwards, you can prioritize your life around them.
- If it seems overwhelming, or quite hard to accomplish, don't worry! Take a breath and look at the small steps that it will take to get there. These small steps will make a huge difference over time.

No one comes out from the womb looking like a body builder, but a rigorous daily routine at the gym can get you there eventually. Therefore, take some time to break the goal into small, doable tasks. Suddenly, the goal seems more manageable and it can even serve as a daily reminder of what you're working towards.

- Make sure to nourish your existing interpersonal relationships and to build new ones. This is a key component for long-term happiness.
- Last, but not least, don't give up or leave things until it's too late. When we feel stressed, it puts us in a vulnerable position and opens the floodgates to a host of unwanted emotions. However, you can avoid any extra stress by dealing with issues head on. Don't ignore them or procrastinate.

### Build Mastery

The term "build mastery" is meant to describe a situation where someone gets to learn new skills. They become proficient in a particular thing.

Once you pin-point some hobbies and activities that you really like to engage in and become skilled in them, this will build your self-confidence. It's a great way to feel capable and resourceful on a regular basis.

It can also be something that you can rely on whenever you feel bored, depressed, or anxious. It might be hard to get into these activities at such moments, but overall, keeping yourself occupied can help to ease any negative emotions that you might be feeling.

The best part is that when you're building mastery, you're constantly in a positive state of mind as you're not planning to fail. You're focusing and expending your energy on something productive. You're planning ahead with the mentality of someone who succeeds.

As time goes by, you will gain more experience and reach more milestones. This will make your confidence levels rise even further and you'll be able to overcome negative emotions more easily because your sense of self will have solidified.

These days, with YouTube DIY videos, it's very easy to learn how to do just about anything under the sun! Macrame, paint pouring, building a table, a raised garden bed, restore furniture, etc. Some things are also very affordable, just add the phrase "on a budget" into your search bar and you'll find there's a way to achieve a goal with limited resources. You can also build mastery with a list of hacks, such as technology hacks, life hacks, etc.

If you don't know where to start, and would like to boost your creativity, you can go to Pinterest, type "how to" in the search bar, and pick one of the predictive text results to see where it takes you!

### Cope Ahead

The term "cope ahead" means anticipating events that you know are going to be hard to get through. It could be a job interview, a presentation, or even an exam. It's important that you prepare for what is to come both on an emotional and on a mental level.

Think about what you need to do so you can feel prepared. Perhaps you have a presentation that you need to give but you're not that great at public speaking. One technique that athletes and business professional alike use ahead of a big game or speaking event is they envision themselves succeeding, knocking it out of the ballpark so to speak. The more invested you are in this vision, the more you'll sense your nervous feelings and self-doubt dissipate. What I mean is to paint as realistic an image as you can.

If you're an athlete, say a basketball player, envision yourself on the court at a critical moment in the game. Imagine yourself mentally and physically immersed "in the zone" and all your senses sharpen. You know exactly what you need to do. You catch the ball thrown in a bit high, but you're skilled so you get a solid grip quickly. You pivot to face the basket and as you do so, a hand comes out of nowhere into your line of sight attempting to block the shot. You plant your sneakers firmly just behind the 3-point line and as you sight the basket, you're able to see past the hand coming toward your face like it's not even there. With your entire body aligned for the shot, you jump up, your arms in perfect position, give a quick release of the wrist, the buzzer sounds, and the ball swishes for a 3. Teammates are celebrating. You won.

For a work presentation or a speaking engagement in front of an audience, envision yourself getting introduced to speak and walking confidently up to the podium. You take a moment to gaze out over the audience and smile. They aren't scary - they're not there to judge or criticize. If anything, they're a bit bored and you're going to blow them away with your presentation because you really know your stuff and you know how to make it sound interesting. Again, imagining yourself mentally "in the flow", speaking to the crowd as if you're speaking to a friend; you're just having a conversation. You feel confident to step away from the podium as you speak and maybe even engage an audience member by asking a question and calling on someone. People are paying attention, you see heads nodding in agreement; they're involved and are interested in what you have to say. This isn't stressful - you're having a good time! You conclude your presentation to a wholesome round of applause and step down. Your presentation was a success.

Imagine at least a couple scenarios that are specific to the event you're planning ahead for, like a difficult conversation with your friend that's likely to trigger you. Imagine yourself being an active and calm listener, an understanding participant in the conversation, the same way you'd like your friend to show up for you. Replay the scenario a few times, maybe changing one minor aspect of the event, but the key is that you envision yourself succeeding at handling every possible version of the event well, being the person you want to be in that moment for your friend. You're effectively training and preparing your brain to achieve the outcome you already expect.

The "ABC" skills are often paired with "PLEASE" skills since the goal is the same - to improve upon your self-care. However, to I separated out "ABC PLEASE" into two separate sections so they're more manageable and easier to remember.

The "PLEASE" skill is another important means of helping lessen your susceptibility to ending up in an emotionally distressing state. The main point is to incorporate elements of self-care into your daily routine which, in turn, can help you to regulate your emotions. With that in mind, the acronym PLEASE stands for:

### <u>P</u>hysica<u>L</u> illness

If you suffer from any physical ailments, it's important to treat them. Take any prescribed medications that have been given to you, and see a doctor whenever you need to.

### <u>E</u>at

Eat meals that are balanced and healthy. Also make sure to eat enough food so that you can sustain and nourish your body. Don't eat foods that might have a negative impact on your emotions. Foods that are high in sugar are a classic example. Beverages like sodas, energy drinks, or sports drinks are to be avoided at all costs because the high sugar content creates a spike in your blood glucose levels. This might feel really good for a while, but afterwards, these levels will plummet, leaving you feeling lethargic and cranky (Spratte-Joyce, 2021).

### <u>A</u>void mind-altering substances

Don't ingest substances that haven't been prescribed to

you by a medical professional, and don't abuse the ones that have. Keep the consumption of alcohol to a minimum, too.

### Sleep

Getting enough sleep at night is crucial. It can help you feel rested and, as a result, you will feel a significant lift in your mood. Have a regular schedule where you get to wake up and go to sleep at the same time every day.

### Exercise

It's important to get a bit of exercise each day. Start small and work your way up from there (Sunrisertc, 2017).

---

## Stretching

As you may know, the body and mind are intricately connected; to emphasize this point, let's take a look at the benefits of stretching. Stretching can actually help people regulate their emotions because when people stretch, it releases feel-good hormones called endorphins. These hormones increase positive feelings and reduce pain (Mascarenhas, 2021).

For instance, the buoyant feelings that you get after a good workout are akin to the feelings you have from spending quality time with the people you love. Below are the main mental health benefits of stretching:

### It promotes relaxation

Stress can cause the body's muscles to tense up or stiffen and goodness knows that there's plenty of stress to go around on a day-to-day basis. This can lead to aches, joint pain, headaches, insomnia, high blood pressure, and even depression. However, doing some stretches can help you to manage stress by releasing the tension in your body. Once again, the endorphins that get released by stretching can also help you to feel calm. This can be a way to get some much-needed relief from stress.

### Boosts energy levels

Stretching is a great way to regulate your metabolism and to boost your energy levels. This spike in energy can make you feel good and helps you to regulate your emotions. The energy boost comes about because stretching improves blood flow and circulation in the body. When that happens, it clears the mind, boosts energy levels, and gets people in a positive frame of mind.

### Increases inner balance

Research has proven that stretching can help people to cope with depression and anxiety and to lift their mood (Mascarenhas, 2021). If combined with breathing techniques (like the ones discussed in Chapter 3), it can also help you to find inner peace and balance. In other words, slow movements that are controlled can get you in a meditative state and calm your mind (Mascarenhas, 2021).

## Humming

There's a book called <u>The Humming Effect - Sound Healing for Health and Happiness</u> written by Jonathan Goldman and Andi Goldman that delves into some very interesting science behind the benefits of conscious humming. Humming is purported to help relieve stress, promote calmness and better sleep, lower blood pressure, release oxytocin, and more. It can be used during a time of stress to help us relax.

The method involves "feeling" the hum, visualizing the hum actually accomplishing what we want it to. Bringing this level of intentionality into your humming can be rather powerful. It can even help relieve physical pain by directing the humming energy (i.e., you can visualize it taking the form of a glowing white healing light) toward the location of the pain (Simon & Schuster, n.d.).

There is much to be discovered in the book, but I will list one exercise below for you to see if it's of interest to you. The recommended timeframe for this exercise is 15 minutes.

1. Close your eyes and take a few deep breaths. Tune into how your body feels and keep taking relaxing breaths for as long as you like.
2. Identify what you're seeking to accomplish, or your intention for this exercise. Perhaps you're feeling totally scattered and want to feel more whole and balanced. Or maybe you've identified a problem area, say an aching knee, and want to alleviate the discomfort.

3. Begin humming and continue for 5 minutes. You're not humming a song but rather focusing on whatever sound comes naturally from within, more like a chant. You can change the pitch at times if that's what you feel like doing and if it helps you direct or project the focus of them hum into your knee specifically or your entire being.

4. Once you've concluded the humming session, sit in silence with your eyes still closed for as long as you like and take note of any changes you experience now or while you were humming.

5. Open your eyes and take a few moments to acclimate. Enjoy whatever the present moment brings - a feeling of relaxation, calm, wonder, curiosity.

There are many ways to use sound as a healing modality. You may enjoy listening to Himalayan Singing Bowls or Crystal Bowls, ocean sounds, binaural beats, spa or meditation music. There's much to discover thanks to YouTube.

# 6

---

# INTERPERSONAL EFFECTIVENESS

Interpersonal effectiveness is a very important skill that people need in order to navigate the complexity of their social relationships. It helps to bring about balance between the relationship they have with themselves and the people in their lives. It also supports a much needed form of equilibrium between their personal priorities and life's demands (Eddins, 2021).

Through interpersonal effectiveness, you will learn how to advocate for yourself and your needs. The goal is to talk about your preferences in a way that is respectful. Struggling with BPD means that, a lot of the time, there is a tendency to be emotionally reactive and not socially effective. This pushes people away, which can be extremely isolating and lonely.

The reason it can push people away is that they might not be able to accept or understand the type of impulsivity that comes with your condition, or the angry outbursts.

If you feel discouraged because you can't seem to connect with people, or feel misunderstood, don't lose hope! With DBT, it is possible for you to cultivate the type of relationships that you want. You will be able to implement effective strategies that can help you ask for what you need, to say "no" when you need to, and to manage conflict.

These strategies are important because they attune you to your environment and the effect you have on others. You'll gain awareness of your behavior and the impact it has on your relationships. This, in turn, is an opportunity for you to find effective solutions to a problem so you can make the kinds of positive changes that are needed for you to have fulfilling and peaceful relationships (Eddins, 2021).

With that in mind, let's take a look at some techniques that can help you speak up in a respectful manner, improve communication, and maintain healthy relationships.

---

## DEAR MAN - to improve communication

This particular technique can assist you in improving your communication skills (Dietz, 2019). If you have an objective that you want to achieve, like asking for a favor or getting someone to compromise with you, the "DEAR MAN" is the way to go and each letter of this acronym is defined below

- **D**escribe the current situation
- **E**xpress your feelings
- **A**ssert yourself
- **R**einforce
- Stay **M**indful
- **A**ppear confident

- <u>N</u>egotiate

Let's take a look at these points in more detail:

### <u>Describe</u>

Explain or relate the situation out loud, in a firm but respectful manner. "Out loud" doesn't mean screaming, but it's simply asking you to verbalize it clearly instead of assuming that the other person can pick up on non-verbal cues.

Only state the facts in a neutral tone. This means you're not making any snap judgments about what happened, whose fault it is, or whether the situation is good or bad (Dietz, 2019). For instance, let's say you want to respond to your child's request for his/her first mobile phone. You can start by saying "I hear that you want a phone and your dad and I talked about it. I'd like to chat about it with you" (Sunrisertc, 2018). No embellishments, no accusations, just simple facts. You're not expressing any feelings on the situation, just making an objective statement.

### <u>Express</u>

Next, communicate how you feel about the situation to the other person. Try not to use "you" statements, but "I" statements. This is less accusatory. The other person won't feel attacked or have to put their defenses up.

It might be tempting to assume that the person you're speaking to knows exactly how you feel, but that's not necessarily true. This is your chance to tell them how you feel in an honest and open manner. For example, you could say "Being only 11, I'm really concerned that you're not ready for for a phone where you'll have complete access to the internet and all those apps. Although you're very mature for your age, it's still easy to make mistakes - especially on social media - that can be pretty tough to bounce back from. You've got so much going on with schoolwork and after-school events and I worry that such a situation could cause extra stress for you".

### Assert

Advocate for yourself by asking for what you need or responding "no" firmly, depending on the situation. To avoid any misunderstandings, be as direct and clear as possible. Perhaps for you, this technique is more about learning how to refuse a request (Dietz, 2019). This is perfectly fine and your right to do so! Using the example above, you could assert yourself by saying something like "Your dad and I together agreed we're not going to purchase a smartphone for you this year" (Sunrisertc, 2018).

### Reinforce

This part is about strengthening your standpoint by highlighting the positive consequences of adhering to your request (Dietz, 2019). If you're declining a request, you'd highlight the negative consequences of them not listening to you.

If you plan to give the person a reward, make sure to stick to your word and deliver it once the desired result is achieved. This is a vital point because people will respond more positively to your request in the future. Keeping in line with the previous example, you could reinforce your statement by saying "We're really proud of you, how hard you're working, and how well you're doing in school. Let's revisit this next year" (Sunrisertc, 2018).

## Mindful

Keep your goal in mind throughout the entire conversation. Don't get distracted by the other person or convinced otherwise (Dietz, 2019). In fact, this could be a sign of manipulation. Don't be afraid to repeat yourself if you feel like they aren't listening to you. Be calm and speak in an even tone.

Unless your 11-year old is a robot, she or he will likely not give up so easily. They may respond by sulking, stomping off, or crying out "but whyyyyyy?!!" and perhaps challenging your decision with the counter-argument that an older sibling has a smartphone or that other kids at school have them. Instead of following your child's misdirection which could lead into potentially muddy waters, you can stand your ground and show that you understand how the child feels. "I know this is upsetting, but as you continue to demonstrate you're responsible, we'll definitely factor that into account when we revisit this next year" (Sunrisertc, 2018).

## Appear Confident

It's no coincidence they say confidence is key. It's the key to having successful relationships and getting the response you want. Be in charge of the conversation and convey to the other person that you are serious by using a self-assured tone and body language (Dietz, 2019). Don't whisper, look down at the floor, twirl your hair (if it's long), or wring your hands. Instead, stand tall, use eye contact, and say how you feel with conviction. As a caveat, don't use words like "maybe", "perhaps", or "possibly" as they open the door for doubt. If you're turning someone down (like your child), confidence projects an air of finality in what you said. Try to stay calm and mindful throughout.


### _Negotiate_

Being confident is good, but don't be so rigid that you miss out on the opportunity to compromise. The other person's needs and feelings matter too, after all. Where appropriate, be willing to be flexible. In other words, be open to give in order to receive.

Look at alternative solutions that can bring you closer to your goal. Be practical about what will work and take a moment to consider things from the other person's perspective. You can even think about asking them for any ideas or solutions that they might have to solve the problem (Dietz, 2019). For example, in keeping with the previous theme, you could try finding out what your child wants to accomplish via the smartphone and see if there's any way you can find a middle ground or way to achieve the goal another way (Sunrisertc, 2018).


You can even use "DEAR MAN" to rectify a discussion, or to initiate a course correction while you're already engaged in conversation. Perhaps the other party is being disruptive, refusing to take no for an answer, or being aggressive. Tell them how the situation is affecting you. Be assertive and explain what changes you would like to see happen so you can have a constructive conversation.

Maybe you could decide to have the discussion later once things have calmed down. That being said, still reinforce your viewpoint and make sure that they know you're not planning to change your mind any time soon. Be mindful and confident as you do all this because succumbing to peer-pressure can be an "easy out" of the difficult conversation at this point and that's not what you want.

You can also think about writing down what you want to say before the conversation even takes place. Write it out in advance and practice with a trusted friend. Maybe there are parts that are particularly difficult for you, or parts that you're more uncomfortable with than the others. Spend some extra time on those until you do feel comfortable with everything that you want to say.

Remember to not be overly emotional or logical about it, but wise (i.e., be a little bit of both by finding a balance between the Rational and Emotional mind). It will help you to stay focused.

Last, but not least, have a clear goal of what you want to achieve when you use this technique. If your goal is clear, your argument will reflect that.

Consider your priorities as a way to clearly determine what you want or need. That way, if you feel a little strung out, you can put off anything that is low on your list of priorities. In addition, it's crucial that you are able to distinguish between your "wants" and "shoulds." Think about the possibility that you might be doing something just because you feel you should (even though you don't really have to do it). Say no to these things.

Typical goals that people have include: standing up for themselves and making sure their viewpoint is taken seriously, refusing unreasonable requests in a way that doesn't undermine them, or resolving conflict.

During the times where a compromise cannot be struck or it simply isn't feasible for you to get what you want, you can turn to the distress tolerance skills that were discussed in Chapter 4, or practice radical acceptance. After all, it's not always possible to get everything you want from others. Even though interpersonal effectiveness can increase your chances of getting your needs met, it's not a guarantee. However, if you can find a creative way to satisfy both you and the other person someway (thereby making it a win/win), that's great.

---

*FAST - to speak with integrity, self-respect*

This particular technique can help you communicate with others in a way that reflects integrity and self-respect (Linehan, 1993).

Keeping hold of your self-respect while trying to balance your relationships can be a huge challenge, but this skill can empower you. It can help you have difficult conversations with more confidence. You get to feel good when it's done because you would've mastered the art of balancing your relationships with keeping your self-respect.

Try to practice this skill when you're not in the throws of a heated argument. That way, you can incorporate it and use it more effectively when the pressure is on. You can even use your pet as a test dummy.

In summary, the whole purpose of the "FAST" technique is to arm you with the skills that you need to grow and take care of your relationships so they can flourish, while at the same time, it also gives you the chance to uphold your values, self-respect, and needs. One cannot be sacrificed at the cost of another.

### (Be) Fair

The aim is to be equitable and fair, not just when it comes to your loved ones, but to yourself, too! For instance, it would not be fair if you had to put the needs or desires of someone else above your own (Linehan, 1993). This includes not being vocal about your own needs or desires and keeping them to yourself.

Advocate for yourself by being firm, not aggressive or passive-aggressive. Speak your truth, while also being mindful of the other person. Listen actively to them and be open to a negotiation or compromise.

The other person is not always going to be accommodating, and that's ok, because you also have the right to hold yourself and others to certain standards. Never accept a situation where your needs are not, at minimum, being considered or honored.

### (Have No) Apologies

Do not apologize if there is no need to do so. Situations that do not justify an apology include making a request, refusing a request, taking up space, having an opinion, disagreeing with someone, or being alive.

Over-apologizing is indicative of low self-esteem and actually perpetuates a mode of self-deprecation. Resentment, self-loathing, and/or self-betrayal are all reasons why people might over-apologize for things (Linehan, 1993). That is not self-respect!

Therefore, if you catch yourself apologizing quite a lot throughout the day, it might be a good idea to think about what you're apologizing for, and whether or not you might've done something that legitimately warrants an apology.

Most of the time, people find themselves apologizing to diffuse or avoid conflict, even though they might not necessarily be wrong. They just can't tolerate the fact that someone else is angry with them and, as a result, they apologize to keep the peace.

That being said, an important point to consider is this: If you apologize for every little thing, the next time it can come across as being insincere should a situation arise where you really want to show remorse.

Be mindful of over-apologizing; catch yourself in the act, and try to break the habit. This will increase your self-respect.

### Stick to Your Values

During the discussion about the "DEAR MAN" technique, there was a section on the need to compromise and negotiate. However, this is not the case when it comes to your values, more commonly known as deal-breakers. Do not sacrifice your own values to appease someone else or to fit in with the crowd.

Doing this is inauthentic. That's why it doesn't feel so good when you do it, because it's like surrendering a part of yourself. Therefore, don't go against the grain of who you truly are. For instance, if a bunch of your friends want to stay out and go drinking till 2 a.m., yet you've sworn off alcohol for personal reasons and have to be at work at 9 a.m. the next day, don't concede! It's clear that this situation isn't what you want or need. Tell them how you feel and come up with other plans, if you need to.

If the people around you expect you to compromise on your values on something that is *so* important to you, then maybe it's time to let them go.

### (Be) Truthful

Don't tell lies, make excuses, or try to stretch the truth. Yes, little "white" lies count, too. Omitting certain facts, or only telling half-truths, can also have deleterious effects.

People tell lies for many reasons; some of them include a fear of confrontation, being worried that the truth might hurt their loved ones, or not wanting to get into trouble. Sometimes, people lie in an attempt to gain control of a situation.

However, telling lies on a habitual basis has a tendency to catch up with the perpetrator. They trip up and forget the lies they tell, or can't keep track of what was said to whom. Don't land yourself in a similar situation; play it safe and just tell the truth. This will give you peace of mind. Anxiety, shame, and guilt will be kept at bay (Linehan, 1993).

It can also strengthen your relationships, because the people around you will actually know who you really are on the inside. If this creates a rift, if they can't handle the truth, then maybe it's not meant to be. Let them go and find people that accept you for YOU!

Most importantly, remember that if you tell lies and the truth gets out, it can be very harmful to your relationships.

---

*GIVE - to maintain healthy relationships*

This technique can help you maintain healthy interpersonal relationships. Let's take a look at what it entails:

### (Be) Gentle

Don't threaten, judge, or attack anyone. That's the first step to start being gentle in your interactions with others. In short, the way you speak and act should not reflect any form of aggression.

Being gentle means that you're treating the people around you with respect and this increases the chance that they will reciprocate your behavior by being gentle with you, too.

Do take note that on occasion you might need to accept a "no" to your requests, and this must be done gracefully. Sometimes the situation will be reversed, but the same rule applies. All these points fall under the umbrella of gentleness.

For example, as a friend, you want to protect someone from making bad life choices and, as a result, you end up expressing your disapproval at a particular desire they have. You do not agree with their viewpoints, but don't wish to put the relationship in jeopardy. In such a case, you can be gentle in your response by saying something like "I'm only saying this out of concern for your well-being. But you are entitled to make your own decisions," or "It is your life so of course you get to choose how you want to live it, but do take what I'm saying into consideration. I only have your best interests at heart" (OptimistMinds, 2022).

### (Act) Interested

You can show a keen interest in what someone else is saying by listening actively to them (i.e., keep eye contact, limit or eliminate any distractions, and don't interrupt them when it's their turn to speak).

Showing interest is crucial when it comes to maintaining relationships or resolving conflict. So when you are engaging with them, don't multitask; be focused. This will show them that you value and respect what they're saying. Going back to the previous example, you can show your friends, or anyone else for that matter, that you're interested in their viewpoint by saying something like "Let's talk about your reasons for choosing this," or "I would really like to know the reasons behind this choice" (OptimistMinds, 2022).

### Validate

Acknowledge the thoughts and feelings of the people around you. Doing this is a great way to maintain any relationship.

Validating someone's thoughts and feelings (without being patronizing or sarcastic) is important because the other person will feel heard and understood. This inevitably shows them that you respect their opinion, even if you disagree with it.

You can show the people around you a lot of support and validation by saying things like "I see that you feel very strongly about this and I respect your sense of autonomy," or "You seem quite passionate about this and I am willing to think about your arguments carefully" (OptimistMinds, 2022).

### Easy Manner

Keep it light, and keep it easy by adopting a laid-back attitude. For instance, smile as much as you can, and keep things light-hearted by using humor. In the appropriate situations, this can ease tension and lighten the mood (Schimelpfening, 2021).

You can show a laid-back manner by using statements like "That's my two cents' worth, but feel free to do what you like with my advice," or "If that's really what you want, then go for it! I've got your back if anything doesn't work out" (Optimist-Minds, 2022).

# OTHER TREATMENTS

## Cognitive Behavioral Therapy

You may have heard of Cognitive Behavioral Therapy (CBT), which has been a traditional form of talk therapy since the 1960s. It was developed by Dr. Aaron T. Beck at the University of Pennsylvania and is still used today as an effective means of treating a variety of mental health related issues. Its central premise is that thoughts, emotions, and behavior are inextricably intertwined. When someone has a negative thought, it results in a feeling of distress/upset which then leads to a corresponding behavior (Guy-Evans, 2022).

If you change the negative thought patterns, you change the resulting emotion, which then makes the resulting behavior more positive. It's not necessarily about validation or acceptance. The approach is more top-down compared to DBT. The different forms of CBT include:

- **Cognitive Therapy:** The aim is to pinpoint and change any inaccurate or distorted thought patterns. This includes emotional responses and any self-destructive behaviors.
- **Multimodal Therapy:** Looks at seven categories that are vastly different but closely linked: behavior, emotions and affect, sensation, cognition, interpersonal factors, substance abuse, and genetics and biological factors (Cherry, 2022). The aim is to treat psychological issues by addressing these areas.
- **Rational Emotive Behavior Therapy:** REBT is a form of CBT that aims to sort through any irrational beliefs that a person may hold. Unlike in DBT, where acceptance, mindfulness and emotional regulation are involved, REBT aims to challenge irrational beliefs. The beliefs are identified, and steps are taken to change them (Cherry, 2022). This is not a warm and fuzzy type of therapy; it's actually very direct and involves persuasion and confrontation on the part of the therapist, who is viewed as a teacher, to aid the patient in discovering their misconceptions themselves (McLeod, 2019).

---

## CBT vs. DBT

You may be wondering what sets DBT apart from CBT. A major component of DBT is that the therapist and patient work together to find a solution. There is a huge gap when it comes to self-acceptance in people who struggle with BPD, so the therapist helps the person address this while using their insight. It is an inclusive, horizontal approach to therapy.

DBT and CBT alike aim to change negative thought patterns and to teach helpful coping skills. CBT, however, has a stronger emphasis on thought patterns and how to reframe them. The thought patterns can fall into a category such as catastrophizing, mental filtering, and overgeneralizing. Once identified, CBT aims to remove those distorted patterns of thought entirely by challenging them head on (Guy-Evans, 2022).

DBT, by comparison, focuses more on balance and the combination of acceptance and change. There isn't a heavy emphasis on changing thoughts. Instead, you become more mindful about what's happening and use specific skills to help achieve a desired result (Guy-Evans, 2022).

As far as time commitment goes, CBT is much shorter - approximately 6-20 weeks. DBT, on the other hand lasts a minimum of 6 months and can even go on for years (Guy-Evans, 2022).

CBT's goal is to recognize distorted thoughts and change them to healthier ones which are more realistic. DBT's goal is to assist in regulating extreme emotions and better the person's relationships with others (Guy-Evans, 2022).

One thing I want to emphasize with respect to all treatment plans where a licensed therapist is involved is this: If you find someone who appears qualified on paper, but isn't quite meeting your needs, seek out another therapist. If you value someone who understands your condition and is very warm and validating but you're sitting in a room with a therapist who is very clinical and process-focused (rather than YOU-focused), there's a better fit for you out there. Consider shopping for shoes - you may find a pair that looks great, but when you try them on, they're incredibly uncomfortable. The pain isn't worth it; look for another pair that'll be a more comfortable fit. There is nothing wrong with this! You don't even owe the therapist an explanation.

Here's a quick run-down of what CBT can be useful for (there's clear overlap with many conditions mentioned earlier in the book that DBT can also be used for): anxiety, depression, panic attacks, phobias, addiction, Bipolar Disorder, eating disorders, substance abuse, grief, stress, ongoing pain, insomnia, low self-esteem, problems in or loss of a relationships (Guy-Evans, 2022).

## Medication

As for medications, they can help manage some comorbid psychiatric symptoms. However, their ability to treat these symptoms should not be taken as a sign that they can treat BPD itself. For example, research shows that prescribed medications like SSRIs (Selective Serotonin Reuptake Inhibitors), which are a type of antidepressant, can help to improve depression and anxiety, but that doesn't mean you're treating BPD itself, only the comorbid symptoms (Chapman, Jamil, and Fleisher, 2022). In short, they can ease some of the symptoms, but you can't tell if there are lasting changes to the overall quality of life because other issues are present.

To top it off, because of their adverse side effects, medications such as SSRIs do tend to create more problems in people who struggle with BPD.

At the time of writing this book, no medications for BPD (i.e., the disorder on its own, not the symptoms) have been FDA-approved.

However, the good news is that recent studies have shown a drastic reduction in the need for medications and medical care if the patient goes for DBT treatment. In fact, the numbers are as high as 90%! (May, Richardi, and Barth, 2016). That's why, in general, psychotherapy is the treatment of choice for people who struggle with BPD, not psychotropic medications (May, Richardi, and Barth, 2016).

---

## Alternative Treatments for BPD

In the end, the central focus of any treatment option for BPD is heavily reliant on psychotherapy. As someone suffering from BPD, you deserve to know what other treatments besides DBT are available to you. The most effective options are listed below for your convenience.

### *MBT/Mentalizing-Based Therapy*

This helps you manage your thoughts and emotions by speaking about and understanding them. A sense of curiosity is fostered in situations that are tense, so you're less likely to make assumptions about the intentions of other people. For instance, instead of assuming that your friend didn't pick up the phone because they don't want to talk to you, you are encouraged to ask questions and to look at things from a different angle. MBT promotes the idea of thinking before you react (Mayo Clinic, 2019).

### DBT/Dialectical Behavior Therapy

DBT focuses on living in the present moment, developing skills for coping with stress, regulating emotions and improving interpersonal relationships.

### TFP/Transference-Focused Psychotherapy

The central focus here is to understand your emotions and interpersonal issues through the patient-therapist relationship (Mayo Clinic, 2019). You get to develop a keen sense of awareness when it comes to any negative behaviors that you may be exhibiting in your interpersonal relationships. However, unlike in MBT and DBT, Transference-Focused Psychotherapy doesn't include group therapy sessions that last for 12 to 18 months (Chapman, Jamil, and Fleisher, 2022).

### STEPPS/Systems Training for Emotional Predictability and Problem-Solving

This is a treatment plan that lasts 20 weeks, includes working in groups that include your family members and/or friends. This is used in combination with other forms of psychotherapy (Mayo Clinic, 2019).

### Schema-Focused Therapy

This type of therapy can be conducted individually or in a group setting. It involves identifying patterns of behavior that may at one time have been useful in helping you survive but now hold you back and cause hurt in aspects of your life. These behavior patterns are transformed into healthier ones through the course of this treatment (Mayo Clinic, 2019).

### Other treatments

Hospitalization or more intensive treatments may be required in extreme cases, or in times of crisis.

---

## Alternative Treatments for Trauma

I want to include two final treatment options that aren't specifically designed for BPD, but people with BPD have reported them to be useful. These two types of therapy are most helpful in the event of trauma, which you may or may not have experienced. Both EMDR and Somatic Therapy are focused on the mind/body experience, meaning there's a targeted effort to understand how the thoughts of a traumatic experience impact what happens in the body and then use a means of distraction to ultimately change the physical response.

### EMDR/Eye Movement Desensitization and Reprocessing

This therapy was designed for the treatment of PTSD but is

also useful for treatment of anxiety, depression, and panic attacks. It involves up to a dozen sessions and the goal is to desensitize an individual, specifically, by dulling the emotional response associated with traumatic memories. This is done with a therapist who immerses the individual in the recollection of said memory focusing on the associated thoughts and sensations that arise in the body. While recollecting this difficult memory, the therapist directs the individual through a series of eye movements (which is the desensitizing process) and then revisits how the thoughts and physical sensations have changed after the eye movement exercises (Clearview Treatment Programs, n.d.).

### Somatic Therapy

Similarly to EMDR, Somatic Therapy is helpful for individuals struggling with PTSD, anxiety and depression, and also other symptoms and conditions. The core of Somatic Therapy is that stressful events are storied in the body and that by helping release those stored energies, an individual will effectively be able to "release" their trauma. The focus is on the physical condition because it's believed that is where the problem lies - in how the traumatic episode "stored" itself in your body. Mindfulness and breathing exercises can be incorporated in Somatic Therapy, along with an individual discovering for him/herself how the feeling of safety and distress show up in the body (Clearview Treatment Programs, n.d.).

# CONCLUSION

## Treatment of Borderline Personality Disorder

Although Borderline Personality Disorder is a single diagnosis, the different forms in which it shows up are as unique as the number of individuals who experience it. When experts started to come to terms with the disorder, it was believed that BPD could not be treated. However, things are different now and research has shown that BPD does respond to treatment.

It's important to get help from a mental health professional if you have BPD because it can ensure that you have a better quality of life and fewer symptoms. For instance, as mentioned earlier, BPD is associated with risky behavior, self-harm, and suicide. This can put you at great risk, but going for treatment can help curb these behaviors.

That being said, don't find just anyone; find a therapist who has a lot of experience with BPD, because the treatment plan has to specifically target BPD. Some therapists might not have the proper training to be able to help you and, as a result, the treatment that you receive may not be as effective.

Treatment options for BPD specifically include: psychotherapy, Cognitive Behavioral Therapy (CBT), Dialectical Behavior Therapy (DBT), or Mentalization-Based Treatment (MBT). Medication can also be involved for comorbid symptoms (such as anxiety, depression, etc), though it will not treat BPD specifically.

All in all, BPD can affect a number of areas in your life - family, work, school, your relationships, and possibly your legal status if you end up getting into trouble, say driving with excessive speed during a moment of extreme distress. Even your physical health can be impacted by it (Salters-Pedneault, 2021). That's why treatment is so important. However, even with all of these obstacles, it's more than possible for you to lead a normal and fulfilling life, as long as you seek treatment and stick to it.

If you're unable to work directly with a therapist at this time, aim to focus on the now and to make small improvements, day in and day out. I mentioned it earlier and will say it again - don't focus on the mountain of stuff in front of you. Instead, focus on getting a small percentage better each day, one way or another, and it will add up!

The tools that you need to achieve this were outlined in the book. You've got it in the bag so why not begin to implement them today? You can certainly do it!

## BPD Recap

BPD is characterized as a personality disorder. As mentioned earlier, personality disorders, in and of themselves, are a cross between your internal perception and external behavior (Salters-Pedneault, 2021). It's the way you view yourself and the world around you. In the case of someone with BPD, these perceptions are quite different from what is normally considered to be socially acceptable and they inhibit this person's quality of life (Salters-Pedneault, 2021).

People with BPD have an unstable sense of self, a fear of abandonment, chaotic interpersonal relationships, and a poor self-image. They can't stick to the plans they make and/or have trouble following through with them. BPD also features angry outbursts and emotional instability, a feeling of emptiness, impulsivity, stress-related paranoid thoughts, and a proclivity towards self-destructive behaviors (Fader, 2020).

### *Unstable sense of self*

When it comes to self-identity, someone who suffers from BPD does not have a stable sense of self. They struggle with their self-esteem and self-image. At one point, they can feel good about themselves, then next thing, they feel horrible.

### *Abandonment*

In the case of abandonment, that is the root cause of the angry outbursts in the first place. The person makes a strenuous effort to avoid feeling like the people around them are going to leave, whether this fear is real or perceived.

### Interpersonal Relationships

Unfortunately, this causes quite a lot of conflict and that's why BPD is characterized by unstable relationships. One moment, the people around them are put on a high pedestal and in the next, that all comes crashing down. Like a pendulum, moods and perceptions of people may swing from like to dislike (or even stronger - love to hate).

### Impulsivity

Impulsivity is quite a pervasive feature of BPD. People who struggle with the disorder quite frequently partake in behavior that is risky and impulsive. This is especially the case when it comes to substance abuse, sexual promiscuity, drinking alcohol, and binge eating.

### Self-Harm

In addition, as mentioned earlier, they have a higher risk of engaging in self-harm, whether it's cutting, burning, or attempting suicide by downing pills (Salters-Pedneault, 2021).

### Emotional Instability

Moods can be all over the place, and each can last for a few minutes to hours. The person's emotions fluctuate quite a lot. They can go from being happy, to sad, to angry in a matter of minutes. The most common types of emotions, in the case of BPD, are fear, anxiety, and anger (Salters-Pedneault, 2021).

### Stress-related Paranoid Thoughts

This has to do with the perception that people are out to harm them. They may fixate on and misinterpret people's intentions as being hostile, even if they are completely innocent. Perhaps someone on the street casually glances their way; this could trigger a response that this person has something sinister in mind.

### Comorbidity

Do remember that, quite often, mental health problems don't stand alone. A single individual can have more than one disorder at the same time. Comorbidity referee to a phenomenon where two or more illnesses co-occur, or co-exist, in the same person at the same time. In short, these conditions feed into each other. For example, you can be diagnosed with Bipolar Disorder, while having problems with substance abuse at the same time. With BPD, if you also suffer from depression, you're referred to as having "comorbid depression and BPD" (Fader, 2020).

---

## People Who Have Difficulty Visualizing

A *lot* of emphasis has been placed on visualization-based activities in this book. If you find it difficult, or even impossible to immerse yourself in a visualization, I'd like to bring to your attention that there is a condition called Aphantasia, often referred to as "Blind Mind". People who suffer from this condition are unable to place themselves "on site" at a past memory, even if it's a significant event, and can't remember visual elements of that event. With eyes closed and using their mind's eye, they don't "see" colors or images - they may just see static. This can be a rather distressing condition and if this strikes a chord for you, you may want to research the condition further.

---

## Final Thoughts

Now that you have familiarized yourself with the strategies outlined in this book, you can put any of them into practice. You know what is best for you and what you need the most right now, so focus your attention on whatever calls to you the most.

Do take some time to investigate various meditation and yoga practices. They have provided *many* people with enormous benefits that they may not have found through any other healing modality.

As a parting message, please remember that your emotions aren't permanent. No matter how difficult things get in the moment, or how impossible it seems, you'll come out on the other side. You always do.

**Last, but not least, if you enjoyed the book, please leave a review on Amazon. This will help others seeking treatment for BPD to find this book and get the benefit of learning the useful tools presented throughout.**

# RESOURCES

Begum, J. (2021 October 7). *Bipolar Disorder*. WebMD. https://www.webmd.com/bipolar-disorder/mental-health-bipolar-disorder

Burgin, T. (2022 February 22). *Hip Openers: Tips, Benefits, Anatomy, and Poses.* YogaBasics. https://www.yogabasics.com/connect/yoga-blog/hip-openers/

Chapman, J., Jamil, R., and Fleisher, C. (2022 May 2). *Borderline Personality Disorder.* NIH. https://www.ncbi.nlm.nih.gov/books/NBK430883/

Cherry,K. (2022 May 16).*WhatIsCognitiveBehavioralTherapy(CBT)?* Very- WellMind. https://www.verywellmind.com/what-is-cognitive-behavior-therapy-2795747

Cirino, E. (2019 December 5). *What Is Splitting in Borderline Personality Disorder (BPD)?* Healthline. https://www.healthline.com/health/bpd-splitting#splitting-examples

Clearview Treatment Programs. (n.d.). *How does Somatic and EMDR Therapy Help People with BPD?* https://www.clearviewtreatment.com/resources/blog/how-does-somatic-and-emdr-therapy-help-people-with-bpd/

Dietz, L. (2017 September 13). *DBT Distress Tolerance Skills: Your 6-Skill Guide to NavigateEmotionalCrises.* Sunrisertc. https://sunrisertc.com/distress-tolerance-skills/

Dietz, L. (2019 November 19). *Objective Effectiveness: DEAR MAN.* DBTSelfHelp.

https://dbtselfhelp.com/dbt-skills-list/interpersonal-effectiveness/dear-man/

Duckworth, K. (2015 October 5). *NAMI Honors Dr. Marsha Linehan, The Creator of Dialectical Behavior Therapy.* National Alliance of Mental Illness. https://www.nami.org/blogs/nami-blog/october-2015/nami-honors-dr-marsha-linehan,-the-creator-of-dia

Eddins, R. (2021 March 1). *DBT 101: Dialectical Behavior Therapy Basics – What is It? HowDoesItWork?* EddinsCounselling. https://eddinscounseling.com/dbt-101-dialectical-behavior-therapy/

Fader, S. (2020 March 5). *How To Recognize Borderline Personality Disorder.* BetterHelp. https://www.betterhelp.com/advice/personality-disorders/how-to-recog nize-borderline-personality-disorder/?network=g&placement=&target=& matchtype=b&a%20d_type=text&adposition

Ferguson, S. (2021 May 10). What's the Difference Between BPD and Bipolar Disorder? PsychCentral. https://psychcentral.com/disorders/bpd-vs-bipolar-disorder

Gatewell Therapy Center. (2020 September 17). *WISE MIND: A BALANCED SYNTHESIS.* https://gatewelltherapycenter.com/2020/09/17/wise-mind/

Glasgow, Dr. J. (2020 May 11). *A Daily Dose Of Dialectics.* Broadview Psychology. http://broadviewpsychology.com/2020/05/11/a-daily-dose-of-dialectics/#:

Gluck, S. (2021 December 17). *Personality Disorders List.* HealthyPlace. https://www.healthyplace.com/personality-disorders/personality-disor ders-info rmation/personality-disorders-list

Gratz, L., Tull, T., and Wagner, W. (2005). *Acceptance and mindfulness-based approaches to anxiety.* Springer.

Greenwald, A. (2020 July 23). *Quick And Easy DBT Mindfulness Exercises*. EymTherapy. https://eymtherapy.com/blog/dbt-mindfulness-exercises/


Guy-Evans, O. (2022 March 9). *What's the difference between CBT and DBT?* SimplyPsychology. https://www.simplypsychology.org/whats-the-difference-between-cbt-and-dbt.html


Hanh, T.N. (1992). *Peace Is Every Step: The Path of Mindfulness in Everyday Life*. Random House Publishing Group.


Horne, R. (2021 May 26). *15 Examples of Dialectic Thinking & How it Can Broaden Your Mind*. Outofstress. https://www.outofstress.com/examples-of-dialectic-thinking/


Krauss-Whitbourne, S. (2018 March 20). *The 2 Major Challenges of Borderline Personality Disorder: The 2 factors that create emotional turmoil in borderline personalitydisorder*. PsychologyToday. https://www.psychologytoday.com/us/blog/fulfillment-any-age/201803/the-2- major-challenges-borderline-personality-disorder


Linehan, M. (1993). *Skills Training Manual for Treating Borderline Personality Disorder*. The Guilford Press.


Mascarenhas, A. (2021 March 5). *The Benefits of Stretching for Better Mental Health. ArnoldM*. https://arnoldm.medium.com/the-benefits-of-stretching-for-better-mental-healt h-70f6c742c838


May, J., Richardi, T., and Barth, K. (2016 March 8). *Dialectical behavior therapy as treatmentforborderlinepersonalitydisorder*. NIH. https://www.ncbi.nlm.nih.gov/pmc/articles/PMC6007584/


Mayo Clinic. (2019 July 17). *Borderline Personality Disorder*. https://www.mayoclinic.org/diseases-conditions/borderline-personality-disorder/diagnosis-treatment/drc-20370242

McLeod, S. A. (2019 January 11). *Cognitive behavioral therapy*. Simply Psychology.
www.simplypsychology.org/cognitive-therapy.html

MedCircle. (2021 February 4). *How to Spot the 4 Types of Borderline Personality Disorder [Video]*. YouTube.
https://www.youtube.com/watch?v=kNi9bEeFOQU

Merz,B. (2020 October 13). *Sixcommon depression types*. HarvardHealth.
https://www.health.harvard.edu/mind-and-mood/six-common-depression- types

Moawad, H. (2022 January 27). *Sleep Patterns in Borderline Personality Disorder*. Psychiatric Times.
https://www.psychiatrictimes.com/view/sleep-patterns-in-borderline-personality-disorder

Moyer, K. (2021 February 19). *Who Benefits From DBT? Who Does DBT Work For?*
Montgomery County Counseling Center.
https://mccounselingcenter.com/2021/02/19/who-benefits-from-dbt-who-does-dbt-work-for/

Olson,A. (2018 December 24[a]). *T4:TheRESISTT Technique*. DialecticalBehaviorTherapy.
https://dialecticalbehaviortherapy.com/distress-tolerance/resistt/

Olson,A. (2018 December 29[b]). *T6:WillingnessvsWillfulness.*DialecticalBehaviorTherapy.
https://dialecticalbehaviortherapy.com/distress-tolerance/willingness-vs-willful ness/

Olson,A. (2018 December 24[c]). *T1:CostBenefitAnalysis.*DialecticalBehavioralTherapy.
https://dialecticalbehaviortherapy.com/distress-tolerance/cost-benefit-analysis/

OptimistMinds. (2022 January 24). *DBT GIVE Skills Scenarios (With Relatable*

*Examples).*
https://optimistminds.com/dbt-give-skills-scenarios/


Pugle, M. (2022 August 21). *The Four Types of BPD.* Verywellhealth.
https://www.verywellhealth.com/types-of-bpd-5193843#:


Richards, L. (2022 March 18). *What is positive self-talk?* MedicalNewsToday.
https://www.medicalnewstoday.com/articles/positive-self-talk


Salters-Pedneault, K. (2020 February 21 [a]). *Dialectical Behavior Therapy for BPD.* VeryWellMind.
https://www.verywellmind.com/dialectical-behavior-therapy-1067402


Salters-Pedneault, K. (2020 March 25 [b]). *How Common Is Borderline Personality Disorder?* VeryWellMind.
https://www.verywellmind.com/how-common-is-bpd-425184


Salters-Pedneault, K. (2020 September 17 [c]). *Mood Lability and Borderline Personality Disorder.* Verrywellmind.
https://www.verywellmind.com/what-is-mood-lability-425304#:


Salters-Pedneault, K. (2020 August 14 [d]). *Mood Swings in Borderline Personality Disorder.* Verywellmind.
https://www.verywellmind.com/mood-swings-in-borderline-personality-disorder-425478


Salters-Pedneault, K. (2021 November 5). *What Is Borderline Personality Disorder (BPD)?* VeryWellMind.
https://www.verywellmind.com/what-is-borderline-personality-disorder-bpd-425487


Schimelpfening, N. (2021 November 5). *What Is Dialectical Behavior Therapy (DBT)?* VeryWellMind.
https://www.verywellmind.com/dialectical-behavior-therapy-1067402


Schultz, K. (2020 October 20 [a]). *Breathing Exercises.* DBTSelfHelp.
https://dbtselfhelp.com/dbt-skills-list/mindfulness/mindfulness-exercises/

breathing-exercises/

Self-Help Toons. (2020 February 25). *DBT Skills: Opposite Action and Emotion Regulation* [Video]. YouTube.
https://www.youtube.com/watch?v=wkxOICjG2is

Schultz, K. (2020 September 12 [b]). *Awareness Exercises.* DBTSelfHelp.
https://dbtselfhelp.com/dbt-skills-list/mindfulness/mindfulness-exercises/awareness-exercises/

Simon & Schuster. (n.d.). *The Humming Effect Sound Healing for Health and Happiness.*
https://www.simonandschuster.com/books/The-Humming-Effect/Jonathan-Goldman/9781620554845#:

Smith, A. (2020 May 16). *Why Do People with Borderline Personality Disorder Feel Empty?* Amanda Smith Treatment and Consultation.
https://www.hopeforbpd.com/borderline-personality-disorder-treatment/bpd-emptiness

Sullivan, K. (2018 November 14). *The power of positive self talk.* AccessibleDBT.
https://accessibledbt.com/power-of-positive-self-talk/

Spratte-Joyce, K. (2021 August 11). *The 5 Worst Foods for Your Mood, According to Experts.* EatingWell.
https://www.eatingwell.com/article/7912675/worst-foods-for-your-mood/

Sunrisertc. (2017 April 24). *Top5DBTSkillstoUseatHome.*
https://sunrisertc.com/top-5-dbt-skills-use-home/

Sunrisertc. (2018 March 26). *DEAR MAN DBT Skill: The Most Effective Way to Make a Request.* Sunrise. https://sunrisertc.com/dear-man/

Made in the USA
Las Vegas, NV
27 August 2023

76701552R00079